WHY
COMPLACENCY
KILLS

STEER Your Future With An Unlimited **IDEA**

HASSAN YOUNES

WHY
COMPLACENCY
KILLS

STEER Your Future With An Unlimited **IDEA**

First published in 2020 by Dean Publishing
PO Box 119
Mt. Macedon, Victoria, 3441
Australia
deanpublishing.com

Copyright © Hassan Younes

All rights reserved. No part of this publication may be reproduced, stored in a retrieval system or transmitted in any way or by any means, electronic, mechanical, photocopying, recording or otherwise, without the prior written permission of the publisher.

Cataloguing-in-Publication Data
National Library of Australia
Title: Why Complacency Kills — STEER Your Future With An Unlimited IDEA
Edition: 1st edn
ISBN: 978-1-925452-14-3
Category: Business/Self-help

The views and opinions expressed in this book are those of the author and do not necessarily reflect the official policy or position of any other agency, publisher, organization, employer or company. Assumptions made in the analysis are not reflective of the position of any entity other than the author(s) — and, these views are always subject to change, revision, and rethinking at any time.

The author, publisher or organizations are not to be held responsible for misuse, reuse, recycled and cited and/or uncited copies of content within this book by others.

Dedication

I would like to dedicate this book to my loving and caring wife Sarifa Alonto Younes and to our four children Adam, Nahda, Ahmad and Dania for their unconditional love and support.

CONTENTS

Foreword ix

Why Complacency Kills and Why You Must Slay it First xiii

Chapter 1: The Sneaky Nature of Complacency 1

Chapter 2: What Causes Complacency? 11

Chapter 3: The Natural Path of Success 19

Chapter 4: The Dangers Lurking in Contentment 27

Chapter 5: Contentment Versus Complacency 35

Chapter 6: Why Routine Can Deceive You 43

Chapter 7: Resisting Change or Changing Resistance 47

Chapter 8: Ovation for Innovation 53

Chapter 9: Communication is the Key 59

Chapter 10: Motivation Versus Inspiration 69

Chapter 11: Are You Living on Autopilot? 77

Chapter 12: Mind Your Company 103

Chapter 13: Internal Laws of Physics 111

Chapter 14: How Big Companies Died from Complacency 119

Chapter 15: How to Tackle Complacency 129

Final Word 137

About the Author 139

Call to Action 141

Hassan's Keynote Presentations 143

Acknowledgments 147

Testimonials 151

End Notes 153

FOREWORD
by Sam Cawthorn

I have been in business for the past two decades and have been an international speaker presenting to thousands of people in more than 40 countries. I have also written multiple bestselling books and as the founder and CEO of the Speakers Institute I have journeyed through challenging times and easier ones alike.

However, in being asked to write the foreword for Hassan Younes' book, it made me reflect back on my professional journey and life path to inspect the times at which complacency may have crept in...

In reading this book, to my surprise, I learned that it is not only the challenging times that present significant risk. Having heard Hassan deliver his key messages as he speaks on the topic of *Why Complacency Kills* made me aware and alert of the inherent risk complacency presents to all of us.

Why Complacency Kills is a groundbreaking book that unearths the greatest dilemma across life and business of our time — complacency. Through relatable metaphors, scientific analogies and personal anecdotes, Hassan Younes takes us on a journey that outlines the hidden issues holding us back and jeopardizing advancement, as he unveils the path to better health, happiness and success in career and business.

Hassan's writing is dynamic and engaging, speaking on a level that appeals to everyone. His book is sure to spark growing interest in the impacts complacency can have for us.

If being at your best in career, business or life is one of your priorities, then you will find it hard to put this book down unless you start implementing some of his suggestions right away in order to improve your life immediately!

From the outset, Hassan outlines the concept of success as being an innate human ability programmed into our DNA. This launching point sets up the parameters for what is to come.

Hassan frames the aspects of behavior that drive our success, he reasons envy and jealousy as natural processes, and in doing so, disarms anyone experiencing these emotions as you flick through the pages ahead. His wisdom as a thinker comes to the forefront through the assertion that complacency essentially hinders our path to success.

Happiness is elusive, he says, and contentment lulls people into achieving less than they can achieve. Younes champions the importance of making change to avoid such stagnation. Innovation of the mind, spirit and thought, force people to grow; and mental inertia is very much a real thing.

Pay attention to the company that you keep, drink up the wisdom shared in the following chapters, as surely when you reflect upon these, as they may well save you from a death of sorts by the real threat that is complacency.

Since you have picked up this book or perhaps it has found its way into your hands by chance, it probably is the right book for you to read right now.

Whether in life or business, the constructs Hassan Younes explores are as relevant to both. Yet, when we look at the slim success rates businesses face these days, this book may hold the insights that can make the difference between make or break of the later.

Understanding just how undermining and dangerous complacency can be to us in all areas of our lives means that moving forward we can be aware, take preventative steps and employ strategies to by-pass the potential threats of complacency. You will uncover why we all need to do this.

Hassan Younes comes from a background spanning aerospace engineering, education, training and success management consulting. Together with being a successful serial entrepreneur for the past twenty years, has made him both the authoritative voice on the topic as well as an international speaker and author.

Hence, when it comes to successfully navigating the pitfalls of life and business, *Why Complacency Kills* is sure to enlighten you as to what to look out for and how to avoid the risks that complacency presents to us all.

In looking back, I wish I could have read this book years ago — it would have saved me some tough times and set-backs on my journey. Needless to say, I cannot commend this book enough to ignite a more positive future you.

Sam Cawthorn

Sam is the Young Australian of the Year, author of multiple internationally bestselling books including *Bounce Forward* and *Storyshowing*. He is a globally recognized speaker and CEO and Founder of Speakers Institute & Speakers Tribe.

> **COMPLACENCY**
> IS A
> **CONTINUOUS STRUGGLE**
> THAT WE ALL HAVE TO FIGHT.
>
> — JACK NICKLAUS

WHY COMPLACENCY KILLS AND WHY YOU MUST SLAY IT FIRST

When I look at our documented human history, I find myself in total sadness as I reflect on the tragic events that have occurred; civil wars, world wars, workplace disasters, natural calamities, transportation "accidents", global and local economic depressions, epidemics, acts of terrorism and famine.

What really gets to me as I read about our history and what makes me feel helpless and frustrated is due to the fact that these tragic events have led to numerous loss of lives. And much of this loss throughout our ancient and contemporary history could have been avoided.

When we read about the corporate failures in our modern history, it can be easily seen that such failures are due to the lax nature of management in the face of changing markets. I prefer to avoid naming specific companies, but most of them failed to evolve or innovate in the face of advancing technologies and markets. Once again, the sad part of this is that these corporate failures and bankruptcies could have been avoided.

Perhaps you're wondering why I have referred to such events as "accidents". You see, I believe that accidents are not the cause of loss of life or economic failures. It is our human nature and behavior that is the cause of loss of life. In other words, it is our human *complacency* that has caused most, if not all the human loss in our history. We, as people, are just too complacent about everything. We are complacent about our own health, our environment, our careers and businesses, diseases and viruses. We are even complacent about our competitions.

This fact of complacency within our human culture is what drives this great sadness within me when I read about the tragic events in the news. Complacency is a very dangerous factor that we all, as human beings, at one point or another may have suffered from. We tend to be "okay" with everything around us, until it becomes too late.

As an entrepreneur, business leader and educational trainer I feel that it is now time I started raising awareness with my colleagues, family, friends and the general public about the dangers of complacency. We cannot be complacent and expect to have the best relationships, a healthy body, effective businesses, successful careers or even positive trade partnerships. If we don't tackle complacency head on, then in one way or another, we as individuals and as a nation, are doomed.

As you read through the book, you will see how easy complacency can kill business, career, health and relationships. I understand this is a bold statement however, I lived it. It's now my purpose to share this information so that you do not have to hit rock bottom like I did in order to understand things must change.

I want you to consider thinking about *complacency as a disease*, that if not caught early enough can and possibly will, take your life. Consider it a virus that creeps up silently and kills anything in its path without hesitation. Are you willing to risk this disease in your life?

It is obvious that you want to reach a point in your business as an entrepreneur where you can take a break and have the freedom to do whatever you like. This is the result most people strive for — but the thing is, the world changes all the time. The environment, the demographics, the customers, the competition, the digital era is **always** changing, and, even though it is great to have a goal to reach ultimate success where you can just leave it all to run on its own, you must still understand there is always work to be done. It may run beautifully for a while, but eventually, your business will become stagnant in ways you could never imagine. And, it is all because of complacency. While the changing world is out of your control, your strategy within your business isn't. In fact, you have **full control**.

This is where this book will help you: to help you recognize if complacency is taking over, and what to do about it.

I hope you benefit from this book as much as I have. I hope it gives you insight and direction into recognizing and combating complacency in your life — wherever that may be.

> ## THE TRAGEDY OF LIFE
> IS <u>NOT</u> FOUND IN FAILURE BUT
> ## COMPLACENCY.
>
> <u>NOT</u> IN YOU
> **DOING TOO MUCH,**
> BUT DOING TOO LITTLE.
>
> <u>NOT</u> IN YOU
> **LIVING ABOVE YOUR MEANS,**
> BUT BELOW YOUR CAPACITY.
>
> IT'S <u>NOT</u> FAILURE BUT
> **AIMING TOO LOW,**
> THAT IS LIFE'S GREATEST TRAGEDY.
>
> — **BENJAMIN E MAY**

CHAPTER 1
THE SNEAKY NATURE OF COMPLACENCY

In 2012, our Childcare business was operating at a capacity of 95% a year. It was the best year we have had in terms of profit and cash flow. Our business was making some decent dollars. Money was flowing through and the profit was soaring. In fact, we were comfortable and relaxed with our business performance, so much so, that I felt it didn't need any attention from us. The idea of marketing and advertising ceased to exist in my head. I mean, why should I waste money on advertising if our business was already running at full capacity? I started to regularly show up late for work and take three-day weekends with my wife.

We were comfortable, lazy and complacent. Three things that proved a recipe for a disaster.

Before I get into how this affected our business I want to explain the difference between laziness and complacency.

Laziness is a state of being where a person refuses to do anything or shows any initiative when they are aware that something needs to be done.

Complacency is similar to laziness, although the difference is that a complacent person is satisfied with what's done and won't drive themselves to do more than what they are doing. This person has become comfortable, and content with continuing to do the same things every day without effort.

If we were to look at this from a formula point of view, complacency would look like the following:

Laziness + Contentment = Complacency

Now, back to the story. I started to manage our business as if it were a self-sufficient machine in which employees simply "did what they were supposed to," where sales grew on trees, and our customers would keep coming back. I assumed that all was great with the business and that we had made it into a permanently successful operation.

As a result, the business suffered from lack of direction, growth and productivity. Competitors began picking off customers, while employees left because of the lack of direction and career growth. It wasn't long before our childcare business took a big hit in its capacity. Quality service disappeared and our business operation went from 90% capacity to merely 34%. Our calculated break-even line was around 45% capacity. Our business was now operating below break-even. It very nearly became one of the 260,000 Australian businesses that close every year.

As the business started running out of money to pay for wages and ongoing expenses, we started using our bank overdraft account. When we ran out of funds from the overdraft account, we started drawing money against our home loan which we had previously paid off. We drew a significant amount of cash from our home loan to fund the childcare operation to keep the business operational.

For 12 months our business suffered at this rate. It was one of the most stressful and dangerous times the business had seen. The bank became concerned about the state of profit and loss of the business so they stepped in and gave us an ultimatum to fix the situation. This forced us to take a good hard look at the business, and we had to make some tough decisions. We needed to do something drastic.

So I stepped back into the business, got back to the basics and shook the whole system up again. This was the wakeup call I needed and was the only thing I could do before losing everything we worked so hard for.

It was difficult to go in and change things around, to up skill or fire the people we knew had outgrown the business (who had also become complacent) and to hire new staff. We also had to take a plunge and be specific and totally transparent with the employees to tell them what we were doing. It was a necessary evil to get in and change everything. It was a process of starting from the bottom again — from scratch — to revive the business.

It was chaotic and crazy and I had to be relentless in the changes. It was difficult, and as part of it, I had to take a good, hard look at myself and understand that I had become complacent and as a result, the business had suffered.

After a very intense 12 months of restructuring, marketing, advertising and improvements around the center, we managed to save our business from the brink of bankruptcy. Capacity started to increase at the center to the point where in the following year, we reached a capacity of 113%! This came with a lot of effort and recognition of what we had done wrong leading up to the crisis.

All this dilemma, hardship and financial difficulty happened because we became comfortable, relaxed and complacent with the level of income the business was generating. Our complacency almost killed off our business.

UNCOVERING COMPLACENCY ISN'T AN EASY TOPIC – BUT IT'S NECESSARY

Complacency and its ill effects are all around us. In fact, the tragic results of complacency is evident in everything that we do. In our modern, documented history, millions upon millions of people have lost their lives in senseless wars, calamities, diseases, road accidents, OHS accidents and other avoidable incidents. Many of these tragedies could be linked to a state of neglect, contentment, laziness and complacency.

The Deepwater Horizon oil spill that occurred on April 20, 2010 in the Gulf of Mexico off the coast of Louisiana, USA, is one example of complacency. The oil spill — which is regarded as the largest marine oil spill in history — was caused by an explosion on the Deepwater Horizon oil rig, which subsequently sank on April 22.

The incident occurred on the night of April 20 after a surge of natural gas blasted through a concrete core recently installed by contractor Halliburton to seal the well for later use. Once the natural gas was released by the fracture of the core, it travelled up the Deepwater rig's riser to the platform, where it ignited, killing 11 workers and injuring 17.

The oil rig capsized and sank on the morning of April 22, rupturing the riser, through which drilling mud had been injected to counteract the upward pressure of oil and natural gas.

The 2011 US National Commission report on the Deepwater Horizon Oil Spill stated that the root cause of the fatal explosion of the oil rig and subsequent colossal spill in the Gulf of Mexico was complacency. The commission report also called out other recurring themes of missed warning signals, failure to share information and a general lack of appreciation for the risks involved.

It's unbelievable when you think about it: A global environmental catastrophe and the unnecessary loss of 17 lives was all due to a culture of complacency within the US government regulators and the oil companies involved in this project.

In 2015-16 there were 130 coastal drowning deaths in Australia. That's huge! According to the Annual National Coastal Safety Report, these drowning deaths were the highest number recorded within 12 years.

According to Surf Life Saving Australia (SLSA), the most common cause of coastal drowning is getting caught in a rip current. On this matter, their research found that while awareness of rips was relatively high, only one in three people could identify one. The report indicated that of the 130 drowning deaths, nearly half occurred at beaches (including nearby rocks and offshore), but no deaths occurred while swimming under lifeguard patrols.

The alarming rise in the number of drowning deaths in Australia prompted a warning against complacency from the Australian Prime Minister Malcolm Turnbull, who stated: "Complacency leads to tragedy, that's why we have to be alert all the time…You cannot take anything for granted."

Large firms and international big brands are not immune from the dangers of complacency. 2010 witnessed the start of the fall of the Blockbuster Video chain. The once giant video rental company filed for bankruptcy. The company never saw the potential profit in online streaming and Netflix and it was dismissed as a potential threat. The illusion of their comfort zone was Blockbuster's main underlying problem. Blockbuster had enjoyed vast success prior and was experiencing large profits. Directors had become wealthy and it seems that the main focuses were being lost. It is important not to allow complacency to disrupt your business.

The saddest part in our lives is when we lose loved ones to terminal diseases or illnesses. We feel helpless and powerless when we see our loved ones fade away to these diseases. It makes it even harder and more regretful if those deaths could have been prevented by early medical screening, diagnosis or treatment. In Australia alone, around 4000 Australians on average die or lose their battles to bowel cancer. Knowing that these deaths could have been prevented by early diagnosis and treatment makes this statistic even more frustrating.

Detection of bowel cancer is simple with today's modern medical technologies. I am not a physician, surgeon or an oncologist on this subject, but our human nature of complacency allows us to neglect our health and our well-being. I am expressing from personal experience, as I have lost my dear brother in law to a terminal disease. At times, I used to blame him for being in that position of not undertaking regular health checks. If he had done the regular health checks, his disease would have been picked up much earlier and possibly been treated more successfully. I remember many years earlier whenever I talked about undertaking regular health checks with him, my brother-in-law would dismiss it and say "I don't want to hear or see bad results". But in the end, he received the result that he never wanted to hear. I miss him dearly. We were best friends and very close to each other. You see, complacency killed my brother-in-law.

Complacency is a serious matter that no person, whether on a personal, work, business or spiritual level should ignore.

While completing early drafts of this book, COVID-19 struck in East Asia — where contraction of the virus quickly spread from an initial handful to a global scale of thousands within few weeks. While writing this book in isolation at home, thousands have already died on our planet from COVID-19: children, mothers, fathers, relatives, colleagues and friends. We had lost our "humanity" in the process with isolation, separation, social distancing, loneliness and fear. As I read the news about this pandemic on daily basis, I could only feel sadness and frustration at the avoidable contractions and preventable deaths that have occurred since this outbreak.

On another detrimental note, businesses across the globe were lost, global companies have collapsed, people lost their jobs, educational institutions have shut their doors and gone online, countries closed their for borders to the rest of the world. What I find interesting is that a tiny microscopic virus has been able to completely transform our way of life beyond what we were able to achieve willingly.

There are opportunities in every situation regardless of impending positive or negative situations and/or circumstances. I believe that if we are unable to recognize opportunities in our living days, then we are totally living complacently blind to every possible opportunity that may be present or pass us. Living in government enforced isolation has been the greatest opportunity for me. Suddenly I found myself having more time to achieve my prior ambitions and even create new ambitions for the future.

It cannot be ignored or denied that it has been difficult for our businesses as the COVID-19 situation unfolded. The fast spread coupled with the deadly effects of this virus created a panic situation with governments, the global media and subsequently had a significant ripple effect on people's mentality and morale. Our businesses, just like other businesses and companies around the country were negatively affected. A drop in customers meant a drop in revenue and in return, a drop in cashflow and profit. You most likely have heard of the saying "save your penny for the rainy days". Well that's exactly what we had done within our businesses. We had contingency plans in place for the rainy days. My philosophy around operating and managing any successful business is that this: Is my business able to survive 6 months without any customers or with a sudden loss of customers? Now if my answer to this question has been "No, it cannot survive" then it meant that I have been totally complacent around my business.

Being complacent around your business does not necessarily mean that it's all about feeling contented and happy in your current positive situation. It's also about preparing and planning for the risks of possible detrimental and unexpected situations to occur in the future. With our contingency plan in place, we were able to survive the economic downturn brought on by the COVID-19 pandemic. In our businesses, we still maintained our staffing levels, we still were able to fulfil our financial duties to our creditors and our businesses are still standing in these difficult times. It's all about looking complacency right in the eyes and staring it down.

Living in isolation, the opportunities for progress, for innovation, for transformation and positive change that I thought of, were in abundance around me. My only concern was that I wanted to get them all done and achieved in the shortest possible time. I felt the time that I had available to develop these opportunities would run out fast. My main focus was to get them done before the isolation period ended. This was for two reasons. The first reason was that I wanted to launch these opportunities when the isolation period was lifted to capitalize on the great prospects of these projects. The second reason was that when the isolation period lifted, I would become busy with the daily operations of normal life.

To the date of writing this book and still living in isolation, I have been able to create five major global projects that have been launched already. Work is still in progress on other projects that are yet to be launched.

When this difficult period of the global pandemic is over, it will set apart two types of people. The complacent and the non-complacent. It will set apart those who took massive action in the face of a dire situation and those who just waited for the "good times" to come back. The real case scenario would be that the complacent type of people will always have the "right excuse" to play. For the complacent people can use the blame game and the blame game always rests on the other side of their fence.

We are not born complacent, it is something that is learned and acquired. It is a skill to be taken up if we choose to. It is up to each one of us to become self-aware of our complacency levels, understand what it takes to change, set ambitions and take action towards a great future of success and achievements.

> THE **MOST DANGEROUS** PHRASE IN THE LANGUAGE IS
>
> *'WE'VE ALWAYS DONE IT THIS WAY'.*
>
> — REAR ADMIRAL GRACE MURRAY HOPPER

CHAPTER TWO

WHAT CAUSES COMPLACENCY?

Complacency exists everywhere around us, and within our own lives. The causes of complacency are many. In fact, so much so, that none of us are immune. The smartest person in the world or the most brilliant multi-million company can fall victim to complacency if they do not remain vigilant.

In many situations, complacency happens over time. It is problematic because people do not see it coming. Complacency is often referred to as the "silent killer" because of this reason: it creeps up over time, and often pounces when we least expect it — or it is too late.

Being aware of the causes and being able to recognize the signs, is therefore critical to safeguarding your business. Let's take a look at some of the red flags or warning signs for complacency.

SIGN #1

You always feel comfortable

It may seem odd but when you go through life without having anything to feel nervous about, or to feel fear of, you become stagnant in your duties, business and life. The "comfort factor" is the number one red flag that you are falling victim to complacency — so keep an eye on it. Of course, no one likes to feel uncomfortable, but the reality is, we must get uncomfortable to move forward. As said by Susan Jeffers, "Feel the fear and do it anyway."

SIGN #2

You haven't learned anything new for a while

Humans are hardwired to learn, evolve and grow, not for boredom or repetition. If you are in a role or routine where everything is the same each day — from the time you turn up to the office, to your coffee break, to tasks and conversations, then you are at risk of becoming complacent. Shake things up a bit and get involved in learning something new, or doing something out of the ordinary.

SIGN #3

You haven't experienced any new challenges for a while

When was the last time you took on a challenge and pushed yourself outside of your comfort zone? It's probably been too long, hasn't it? This sign goes hand-in-hand with the previous two signs and is often accompanied by the feeling of "being stuck" (sign six on the next page). Outside your comfort zone is where all the exciting things happen.

SIGN #4

Your routine has not changed

While humans are creatures of habit, sometimes there can be too much repetition. If your life follows a certain routine which you haven't stepped outside of due to fear or laziness, then complacency may be the reason.

When we get stuck in the day to day, we fall victim to "going through the motions" — stuck on autopilot without conscious thought, suppressing our creativity and disempowering ourselves in the process.

SIGN #5

You reject change

Are you rejecting change in your life? In your business? Are you too comfortable and too afraid to shake things up? If you are the type of person who refuses to change, then you may be falling victim to complacency. Typically, people aren't comfortable with change — but it's a failproof mechanism for preventing a slip into complacency. Ask yourself, "Why does change scare me so much?" and see where your answer takes you. You may be surprised by your answer and it may be enough to get you thinking about doing something different.

SIGN #6

You are stuck

Being stuck means you are not considering other ways to look at a situation and doing the same thing every day. Whether in business, personal life, relationships or life in general, if you have found yourself saying, "I'm stuck and don't know how to fix it" then you may have fallen into complacency. This is an important time to take a step back, re-evaluate your life, look at what needs to change and then make a plan to move forward (more on that later).

SIGN #7

You rarely try anything new

This follows on from the previous concept of being stuck. If you never try anything new, you'll never discover what is fun or could be working better for you.

This is the dangerous complacent part of life, and our routine ways of living are often to blame. If you feel this may be you, start with something small, like picking up a book in a completely different genre that you are used to reading. This will automatically take you out of your comfort zone and create something new in your life.

SIGN #8

You are predictable

Predictability is a killer. While being predictable can be good, especially if you are good at something, predictability in business will not only hurt you, it will become boring and you will be risking losing precious clients. To avoid this trap, see where you are predictable in your life and start planning on how you can change it. You can even chart your activities in a diary to see how predictable you are.

SIGN #9

You have no ambition

If you are completely lacking ambition, then this is another way you can recognize complacency overcoming you in your life. Some people like to do the mundane tasks and not have anything to look forward to. I know this is not you though (otherwise you would not be reading this book!). Ambition is something that happens innately, so, find something that gets you excited and run with it.

SIGN #10

You have spiritually, emotionally and mentally stopped growing

Have you ever met people who have absolutely nothing happening in their life, who have the same conversations and feel there is always something missing? Do you recognize this in yourself?

You never want to stop growing. Obviously, physically there is a limit to how much we grow, however, spiritually, emotionally and mentally, we want to continually be challenged to grow and learn. In doing so, these learnings will be reflected in our communication and through our leadership qualities in our business.

> WE ARE WHAT WE REPEATEDLY DO.
>
> **EXCELLENCE,** THEN, IS NOT AN ACT, BUT **A HABIT.**
>
> — ARISTOTLE

Hassan is sharing more in his INTERACTIVE book.

See exclusive videos, audios and photos.

DOWNLOAD it now at **deanpublishing.com/ whycomplacencykills**

CHAPTER 3

THE NATURAL PATH OF SUCCESS

As humans, we achieve many milestones. From biological milestones, such as brain development, immune system, or growing teeth, to physical milestones such as developing skills to crawl, run, or speak. We experience personal milestones such as completing education, entering, or leaving relationships, achieving new hobbies, financial milestones such as business deals, new contracts, or meeting a KPI. Success is simply that: achieving a milestone.

Success is embedded into our natural human lives. It is part of who we are as human beings. Success is in our DNA, in our thoughts, in our behavior and in our actions. To unpack this, let's take a look at the human body.

If we look at our biological structure, we find that all our organs work systematically and successfully in perfect coordination with each other.

Our brain is the core processing unit that controls and keeps our bodily organs, tissues and cells working and operating. Its purpose is to ensure the successful operation of all our internal organs and muscles.

Now, most of our body is made of muscles and muscles need oxygen to function. This process starts with the lungs: as we inhale air, the air tubes in our lungs extract oxygen elements from the air and absorb this oxygen into our blood cells. At the same time, carbon dioxide (CO_2) is extracted from our blood cells into the air that we exhale. The oxygen replenished blood is then sucked out of the lungs and into the heart, due to the blood pressure created by the heart pumping. The heart then pumps the good blood into all the organs, tissues and muscles of the body, thus, ensuring all our muscles have a constant and regular supply of oxygen.

Our blood also carries cells that fight any foreign bodies such as bacteria. Our kidney's function is to purify our body from all toxins, impurities and excess minerals that may be present in our blood. This is done by filtering these impurities from the bloodstream that enters the kidneys into the gallbladder to be discharged as urine. Our liver is the organ that produces and regulates the supply of blood. It is also the organ that extracts all nutrients from the food that we eat in our digestive system.

In addition to physiological operation, other survival mechanisms are present in our body. These are found in our stress hormones: cortisol, adrenaline and norepinephrine. Our stress hormones are what gets us up in the morning to start our day. When we run around completing our daily tasks or chores, driving our cars to work, or going for a jog or workout at the local gym, are a result of adrenaline and cortisol being injected into our bloodstream by the separate glands above our kidneys.

It is these stress hormones that give us the extra boost of energy to survive and strive in life.

You may wonder why I am covering so much on our biological functions. You see, success is built inside our DNA. Our DNA, biological composition and nervous system operate to make us succeed. To survive. This is part of our natural path to success in life. Our bodies do all this without us thinking about it. It truly is magnificent knowing that we are programmed for success!

Another reason success is part of our natural life is that we are driven by thoughts and emotions. This is a natural human phenomenon.

This is about emotions such as envy and jealousy. Envy is when you desire something you don't have, and jealousy is when you fear losing something you *do* have. We all feel envy from time to time, no matter how much we want to believe we are above it. Envy is a complex cluster of feelings that stems from an extremely basic desire: We want what we believe will make us happy, or what we see someone else has.

In normal social structures, envy and jealousy are considered a bad and undesirable social behavior. But this is not always the case. Envy may instill the seed of desire to achieve or succeed inside ourselves. Jealousy will drive us to protect what we have, to remain successful in what we achieved or gained

Similar emotions are also at play, when we interact with people who have achieved some great things in life, such as securing an excellent job, or promotion, or who drive a brand new car, or have a perfect lifestyle, it creates an emotion of mirroring this person in their success. In simple terms this behavior is called match and mirroring and is instilled in us as part of our thinking and behavior.

To give you a personal example, when we started our travel agency business and we already had our childcare business in operation, we engaged a business coach/consultant to guide us in our business matters. For our first meeting, the consultant arrived in a brand-new Mercedes-Benz CLS coupe. A car that belonged to his lifestyle of luxury. Now at that time, I had never driven a luxury car, let alone an expensive one. I looked up to his lifestyle, at his status and immediately wanted to mirror his "success". Although he never spoke of his achievement as a successful entrepreneur I wanted to be "successful" just like him. Fast forward many years, and I'm grateful to share that I too, have achieved that vision. Now, I'm the person driving a new Mercedes-Benz.

Self-recognition is another innate emotion — and behavior — that we share. From birth, to learning to crawl, walk or talk we seek recognition for our achievements. The small praises that we used to get as babies or toddlers gave us the encouragement, we need to try more, and achieve more. That is why in early childhood education there is great emphasis on positive interaction and positive communication when young children achieve something. As we grow older, we love to get those words of praise from our parents or teachers. Recognition for our achievements from others creates that joy and self-belief, that "can-do" positive feeling.

This need for self-recognition drives us indirectly to strive harder, to achieve more in the hope that we will get that recognition from others in our environment. Our self-esteem seeks external recognition for the things we do, whether be it on a family level, work level or even on a public level. This is yet again another part of human nature that is present in each of us. The need to be recognized, is a driver for us to be successful in life.

Considering all the above about our human nature and biological structure, one element that is present in our nature is that we believe money is a symbol of success. To many people, success is measured by how wealthy people are. A common mentality exists that "if I have lots of money, I am successful."

While this may, or may not be true, money and financial status is often a driver for many people towards success. Love of money and the understanding that money can buy material things in life such properties, cars, expensive signature clothing or even happiness, is a key element that guides people towards becoming successful.

Knowing what we know about success being hardwired, it shouldn't be hard to achieve right? Unfortunately, this natural path is hindered by one powerful obstacle: complacency.

How does complacency interrupt this flow? As mentioned in chapter one, there are many signs that indicate when complacency is taking over your business. Apple is a great example to illustrate how this works in practice.

While Apple is highly successful, their complacency red flags are flying high. First, they have become predictable. People now expect the "new and updated" iPhone every September. This *pattern*, is dangerous, as they are no longer *unpredictable*, or *surprising* consumers. People now *expect* a new iPhone every year, rather than be excited by the prospect.

Recognize the key words in this statement. If this sounds like you and your business has slowed, lacks goals or a clear vision, waning on inspiration or has hit a plateau (i.e. comfort) then take it as sign of danger. If you are no longer excited about what is coming out of your business, then your customers are not excited, which then creates stagnation.

Stagnation in a business is dangerous — let alone in life in general. It can be recognized as hitting a plateau where everything is flat-lined: your knowledge, challenges, and life.

It's when everything becomes boring, there is nothing new to experience and "auto-pilot" is switched on. This is how complacency begins and this is how it started with me. The result? Your business will fail if you don't do something different.

Imagine for a moment that our scientists who work diligently to create vaccines and cures for diseases decided one day, "That's enough. We have a lot of vaccines, let's all relax and take our long service leave." Or, imagine the government decides to stop engaging in foreign affairs because they think "The country is doing okay." These are all scary thoughts, aren't they? You may be thinking, "That will never happen" but it does, it has and will again, unless people begin to realize that complacency is a silent disease and may strike anyone, regardless of race, success, gender or how much money they have.

While success is something we can all strive for, it is also something we need to work for. Not just individually but collectively. The success of your business depends on more than just you: your employees, systems, vision, goals and mission statement all contribute. Which is why if something isn't working, you need to identify it pronto, to minimize risk.

It may not be an easy task, but if you want to be successful and continue to be successful, then you must be drastic in your changes — because change is inevitable and you must be flexible and keep up with the change otherwise you will be swallowed whole and your business will not survive. It is an non-discriminatory disease and anyone is a likely candidate, unless you arm yourself with the knowledge and tools I'm sharing in this book.

Success is ongoing and requires work. We are built for success, not to sit on our backside, think about success and hope or pray that it will find us. If it were that easy, nobody would be worried about making money, and nobody would be inspired to create, or achieve.

Being successful is so much more than just money. It is important to see it from every aspect to survive in this ever-changing world and to recognize if complacency has started affecting your success — whatever area of your life. You must become brutal in recognizing where complacency has begun to spread within the business and within your life and tackle it head on. Sure, it may get messy and tricky for a while, but in the end it will be worth it.

CASE STUDY

Success could be in your DNA, according to research. A genome-wide association study conducted on more than 20,000 people in the UK, US and New Zealand found those with certain genetic variations got further in education, earned more money and had better careers, than those who didn't.

The study completed by the Duke University School of Medicine in Durham, North Carolina, followed participants from childhood into adulthood and social mobility is partially written into our genes — which can make us successful or not.[1]

---

1. Belsky, D. W., Moffitt, T. E., Corcoran, D. L., Domingue, B., Harrington, H., Hogan, S., ... Caspi, A. (2016). The Genetics of Success: How Single-Nucleotide Polymorphisms Associated With Educational Attainment Relate to Life-Course Development. *Psychological Science*, 27(7), 957–972. doi.org/10.1177/0956797616643070

> **SUCCESS**
> IS <u>NOT</u> FINAL,
>
> **FAILURE**
> IS <u>NOT</u> FATAL:
>
> IT IS THE
> **COURAGE**
> TO
> **CONTINUE**
> THAT COUNTS.
>
> — WINSTON CHURCHILL

CHAPTER 4
THE DANGERS LURKING IN CONTENTMENT

While the notion of "happiness" — what it is, what it's made of and how to measure it — is yet to be empirically defined, there's no denying that we all seek happiness in one way or another.

Happiness is highly subjective. Not everyone finds happiness in the same ways or by doing the same things. Which is often why when we ask ourselves if we are happy, we hesitate in our answer. Our happiness works on different levels and can be applied to different things. For example, I might be happy with my job, but unhappy with the car I am driving, or the relationships that I'm in.

We all possess certain degrees of happiness. In general, there are three levels of happiness that we can experience.
- **Level one**: Short term positive emotions
- **Level two**: Wellbeing
- **Level three**: Self-fulfillment and purpose

Level one represents short-term positive emotions and/or momentary feelings of joy. This can also be defined as "simple pleasures". Some examples of level one happiness is having a good meal, watching a great movie, listening to beautiful music, or enjoying sex.

We can easily detect or observe this level of happiness in people because of the immediate feelings or emotions they experience. During brain scans, these types of emotions are easy to measure and compare as certain parts of our brain are active when we feel these emotions.

This level of happiness does not last very long and we will return to our "baseline" or normal mental state quite quickly. This level is about the immediate feelings of happiness from certain stimuli.

Level two happiness is more about judgments and thoughtful considerations. Level two happiness is about our well-being. To understand this second level of happiness we need an assessment that stretches beyond the momentary feelings of level one. Questions about well-being normally work at this level. For example, if you were asked about how you have been, or how your career is progressing, or even just general questions about how happy you are with your life, your answer will reflect a level two assessment of your happiness. You would not take into consideration the good meal you had for lunch, or the nice movie you watched in the cinema.

At level two happiness there is a tendency in our nature to compare our well-being situations with other people's well-being, or against how we have felt in the past.

You have probably come across international surveys or research that may claim people in country A are happier than people in country B. This type of research refers to level two happiness measured through various surveys in both, country A and country B.

Level three happiness is about the level of self-fulfillment or purpose. The happiness we feel when we achieve our full potential. This level of happiness is about our higher meaning in life and has to do with self-realization. This is illustrated in Maslow's hierarchy of needs where self-actualization is at the top of the pyramid.

It is more complicated to measure level three happiness than the previous two levels. Generally speaking, people who experience high level three happiness live more in harmony with their deeper values. People experiencing this level of happiness tend to have fewer inner conflicts because they often feel that they are fulfilling their purpose in life and achieving greater things for the wider community and within society.

Now that we have a clear understanding of all three levels of happiness, we can open the discussion on happiness further and discover its effect on our personal and professional lives.

People often associate the words "content" with "happiness" — and while both emotions are parts of the same coin, they are not the same. The Oxford dictionary defines contentment as, "a state of happiness and satisfaction". The word "state" in this definition is important to note, as it refers to a state of mind or emotions that determines whether a person is content in their situation.

To look at a practical example, let's consider person A who may be content with X level of financial income while person B living in the same country, suburb or town may not be content with the same X level of financial income. Why? Because contentment is a personal choice that is directly linked to the level of happiness or satisfaction that we have.

When we choose to be content, then essentially, we are choosing to accept our situation. Contentment brings about harmony and calmness to our inner self by settling for what you have or what you are. In turn, inner calmness makes us feel we are in control of our situations. It makes us feel secure. But inner calmness caused by contentment that we chose, will make us oblivious to the potential opportunities and abundance that may be present all around us. Which is often a trap people fall into. So why do we accept to be less than satisfied with our levels of happiness and subsequently choose to be content?

Many faiths and cultures seek and value contentment as part of their teachings and guidance. Various faiths enforce the need for their believers to be content with what God or the universe has given to them. The teachings of various faiths are to happily accept what is given to you. This is not in disagreement with any faiths or cultural teachings, but there are also other teachings that these faiths endorse and encourage. For example, to strive to do your best in life. To help those in need or who are disadvantaged. To be kind and supportive. To learn and teach others and guide them into the righteous paths. In the Christian, Islamic and Judaism faiths there are specific teachings that encourage us to ask for what we don't have. "Ask and you shall be given".

Although contentment and inner calm is encouraged in many faiths and cultures, asking and striving for more than what we have is also encouraged. In fact, if we analyze the various scriptures and texts of the main faiths, we find that it is compulsory to ask the supreme Creator for more. We cannot simply accept our situations and choose to be content based on the teachings of our forefathers. Spiritually, it is permissible to ask and strive for more in life so we can help the poor and the disadvantaged and support the positive growth of our society.

A dangerous aspect of contentment is it makes us vulnerable to our environment. You probably would have heard of the phrase "sitting ducks"? This phrase comes from hunting and basically translates to mean that a sitting duck on the water is an easier target than a flying duck. Think about it: when flying around high in the sky, ducks are difficult to shoot at. However, ducks seen floating, or "sitting", on top of the water as they search for food become especially vulnerable to hunters because they are still. Content as they bob searching for food, but an easy, vulnerable target.

When we are content in our situations, whether they be personal, business or financial, we become "sitting ducks". We become easy targets and vulnerable to our environments. Content people are vulnerable to their environments. If we do not evolve to improve, innovate, improvise, transform or change our situations for the better we are like sitting ducks to everything around us. An employee not constantly improving his/her professional skills or knowledge, becomes a target of demotion or unemployment. A lecturer at university without involvement in ongoing research in his/her field may become the target of replacement. A business not adopting the concept of innovation and constant improvement becomes a victim of the competition. A student not constantly studying or reviewing study material will not receive the grades hoped for. All these examples have one thing in common: contentment.

While there is a place for contentment in your life, it's important to recognize that when it comes to business, you cannot afford it. It is a danger and disaster waiting to happen, and a front row seat to complacency. Understanding the levels of happiness outlined in this chapter will give you a clue to see where you are sitting on the complacent — contentment scale and where you have opportunity to change. Ask yourself; are you a sitting duck, just waiting and taking it too easy or are you the duck who is flying around, happy but working to survive?

CASE STUDY

Louis Mosca, Executive Vice President and Chief Operating Officer of American Management Services Inc wrote an article for Forbes about what it is like to work with complacent leaders. Based on his experience working with a commercial printing company that generated $16 million per year in revenue, he identified issues with the company's leadership:

"*The owners would regularly show up late for work, take three-day weekends, and play golf two-to-three days per week. They managed their business as if it were a self-sufficient machine.*"[2]

Those owners did not fix their complacent ways. Just four years after Louis started working with the business, the company wound down. All that is left is an empty building.

---

2 Mosca, Louis. (Published online November 30, 2017) "complacent-leadership-might-be-killing-your-business". Forbes Magazine, https://www.forbes.com/sites/louismosca/2017/11/30/complacent-leadership-might-be-killing-your-business/#4ff05f3ef708

But it's not just small businesses that are at risk. Barnes & Noble's famous scuffle with Amazon in the online book space shows that. The company believed that its brand name alone would allow it to move beyond Amazon's emerging empire. As the company's CEO, Steve Riggio, stated:

"Clearly, we thought there was going to be room for us and Amazon."

There wasn't.

Barnes & Noble waited far too long to get into the online book space. Their assumptions that they had powered past the competition, proved incorrect. Now, Amazon is the market leader in that space because its leaders showed the hunger and drive to make it happen.

This is what happens when you become complacent. You lose the drive that spurred you on to achieve amazing things. You lose sight of your goals and start to tolerate poor performance within the business. Your team becomes less productive and the key players leave. Slowly but surely, complacency destroys everything that once made your business great.

> **COMPLACENCY IS THE DEADLY ENEMY OF SPIRITUAL PROGRESS.**
>
> **THE CONTENTED SOUL** IS **THE STAGNANT SOUL.**
>
> — AIDEN WILSON TOZER

CHAPTER 5
CONTENTMENT VERSUS COMPLACENCY

In our previous chapter, we talked about contentment and its effect on our lives. The secret side of contentment is that it normally leads to complacency. During my early years as a trainer and lecturer, I was amazed by how many of the participants in my sessions were not aware of what complacency was. They did not have even a simple understanding of what complacency meant.

So, what is this thing we call complacency? The Cambridge dictionary, defines complacency as "a feeling of calm satisfaction with your own abilities or situation that prevents you from trying harder." The Merriam-Webster dictionary provides a slightly different definition; stating that complacency is, "self-satisfaction especially when accompanied by unawareness of actual dangers or deficiencies." In both definitions, there is a link between contentment and complacency. At times, it can be difficult to distinguish between contentment and complacency because they both involve inner calmness or self-satisfaction. Both of which, are normal states of being in our lives.

We all need calmness and rest. It is in our biological composition that our brain cells and organs require rest and relaxation for at least eight hours a day. These moments of rest and relaxation require physical calmness. Inner calmness, however, is of a psychological nature. Usually, people achieve these states through meditation, or prayer, however, there is a risk that this inner calmness is a result of contentment and complacency. Which is where the danger presents itself because this type of inner calmness will shield you from your surrounding environment for a long period of time. It may create a safety-net bubble around you, making you feel secure and safe.

Total inner calmness makes a person stagnant in their thinking, in their actions and in their activities. Total inner calmness provides a person with a comfort zone that can be dangerous because it creates hatred or dislike towards change and innovation.

A tragic incident that provides an example on the seriousness of complacency is the crash of Colgan Air flight 3407 on February 12, 2009, near New York, USA. This crash killed all 49 people on board the flight and one person on the ground. Investigations into the matter attributed cause to complacency. In fact, the Chairwoman of the National Transportation Safety Board (NTSB), Ms Deborah Hersman, stated it was the pilots' "complacency and confusion that resulted in catastrophe".[3]

The findings revealed that Captain Marvin Renslow and co-pilot Rebecca Shaw were distracted and unlikely to have realized they were traveling at dangerously low speeds. The flight lost 50 knots of airspeed in 20 seconds while they chit-chatted on approach to Buffalo Niagara International Airport. A cockpit voice recorder transcript shows Renslow and Shaw discussing careers and her lack of experience flying in icy conditions during the plane's final minutes, even after they had noticed a buildup of ice on the windshield and wings.

When we think about complacency, we can easily identify that there is an element of ignorance and denial. This is part of self-satisfaction. Self-satisfaction is when our thoughts start to create beliefs of how well things are going for us personally or how there is no need to initiate any changes. Our thoughts and beliefs become so strong about our situation that anything deviating from those thoughts gets filtered out and ignored. As our thoughts ignore reality, the danger or risk becomes closer and ever present. At times it could be too late to take any corrective measures or action to avoid these dangers or risk.

There are thousands of books and articles on limiting beliefs and how to avoid them. It is worth mentioning that limiting beliefs, in some cases, form the foundation of complacency. If we look at some examples of limiting beliefs it becomes evident how they create complacency.

An employee of a firm may have the belief that "My boss doesn't want to help me with my career development." This type of belief automatically shuts down the desire of the employee to increase his/her performance or become creative.

---

3 James, Frank. (Published online February 2, 2010). "Colgan-Buffalo Plane Crash: Errors Began Pre-Flight,". National Public Radio NPR. https://www.npr.org/sections/thetwo-way/2010/02/colganbuffalo_plane_crash_erro.html

Shutting down the desire to improve creates contentment and complacency around improvement.

Another workplace belief may be that "Asking for help is a sign that I'm not good at my job." People with this limiting belief never ask for help or guidance to do their job in a better way. Being afraid to raise your hand for clarification or further understanding makes a person accepting of their abilities as "good enough" to get the job done. Therefore, complacency sets in.

In business, managers are faced with many challenges in their role. However, at the same time, a manager's beliefs play a big part in how well the business performs in the market and how profitable it is. A limiting belief that may exist in a manager's mind could be: "If we spend on advertising, we may not sell as expected". With the fear of "loss of investment" in marketing, the manager would not do an advertising campaign. Thus, accepting the current situation without advertising and falling victim to complacency, while the competition is dominating the market with their initiatives.

Limiting beliefs are directly linked to complacency.

We have all heard of the story of the ostrich (of if you're in Australia, the emu) sticking its head in the sand. This saying revolves around the belief that the African Ostrich and Emu both stick their heads in the sand to avoid predators or dangers. Ironically, this is not true and merely a myth (besides, if this did happen, surely the ostrich would die of suffocation!)

Given what we know about ostriches, though, it is easy to see how this myth started. Ostriches are the largest and heaviest living birds on Earth. Despite being two meters tall and weighing as much as 150 kilograms, ostriches have relatively small heads. When nesting, they dig shallow holes in the ground to use as nests for their eggs, which they cover with sand. They use their beaks to turn their eggs several times each day. From a distance, an ostrich leaning into a hole to turn an egg can easily look like it's burying its head in the sand.

You may wonder what this has to do with complacency?

In 2009 just before the Global Financial Crisis (GFC) hit, our childcare business was doing great. Profit was the highest we had ever achieved. Our childcare business was operating at full capacity. It was the best year in revenue and sales. When the GFC arrived, it was a huge event in the Australian news and media. At that time, I thought the financial crisis was a global issue and would not affect medium sized Australian businesses. I went into denial and ignorance, thinking that our business would not be affected. However, within three months of the financial crisis, our business started to feel the ripple effect. Our customers started to reduce their business with us and as a result, our sales and revenue dropped. Needless to say, our profit took a sharp dive and our once prosperous booming business entered survival mode.

Earlier on we covered how denial and ignorance fall under the complacency umbrella. Well, this is what occurred. I was in a state of denial and totally ignorant about the global situation. You will find that complacent people tend to lie to their inner self about their situations or abilities. They tend to ignore their own abilities for bigger potential. With their denials and ignorance, complacent people hope for the best to happen. Just like the ostrich sticking its head in the sand, or the sitting duck in the pond, complacent people hope that any adversities will pass by without any ripple effect.

While our business took some time to recover, it never went back to where it was. The point I am making with this is that I learnt the hard way, what denial and ignorance look like.

And because I ignored the effects of the crisis and went into denial, I wasn't able to prepare myself for the fall out. It is highly likely that many people can go from a highly adaptable state of dissatisfaction to experiencing complacency if they are not constantly vigilant. So keep your eyes open and stay alert, because your business is not immune.

CASE STUDY

Did you know that only 12% of the original Fortune 500 companies from 1955 are still in existence today? It is staggering!

What caused this fall? While their stories might be different, they have one thing in common: contentment, leading to complacency.

These companies failed to recognize threats and respond to factors in their marketplace, leading them to failure.[4]

---

4 Perry, Mark. (October 20, 2017). "Fortune 500 firms 1955 v. 2016: Only 12% remain, thanks to the creative destruction that fuels economic prosperity." The American Enterprise Institute. https://www.aei.org/carpe-diem/fortune-500-firms-1955-v-2017-only-12-remain-thanks-to-the-creative-destruction-that-fuels-economic-prosperity

> I REALLY TRY TO PUT MYSELF IN UNCOMFORTABLE SITUATIONS. **COMPLACENCY IS MY ENEMY.**
>
> — TRENT REZNOR

> **I WILL NOT** ALLOW YESTERDAY'S **SUCCESS** TO LULL ME INTO **TODAY'S COMPLACENCY,** FOR THIS IS THE GREAT FOUNDATION OF FAILURE.
>
> — OG MANDINO

CHAPTER 6

WHY ROUTINE CAN DECEIVE YOU

Humans are creatures of habit. We all have routines. In fact, we like routine. Ordinarily, routines can be useful: they help us feel in control, give us structure, assist to get things done, and make us feel comfortable. Our routines, developed through doing the same actions time and time again, become automatic; easy.

Which is why most people may think they are in a good place when you have a solid routine. Knowing what to expect, not having to think, auto-pilot being switching on…it can only be a good thing right?

No. In fact, routines are highly dangerous. Think about the process for a moment. Each day, you get up at the same time, have the same thing for breakfast, drive the same route to work. You walk into the same office, order the same coffee at

10am, see the same people, have the same meetings, and leave by 5pm. Going about what is "another day".

But the problem with this, is we become too familiar, too comfortable and we start wearing blinkers. We develop unconscious (automatic) habits. Our awareness and thought, only seeing, or thinking what we have conditioned it to see, based on our routine.

Having a routine can create a false confidence in what you are doing. There is no challenge to take on and new thoughts aren't being created, and our behavior happens without conscious awareness. Have you ever found yourself at work without remembering the drive home. This is a great example of how our routine can "blind us". In fact, many road accidents and workplace accidents happen this way. The familiarity created by routine, doesn't allow us to predict or anticipate changes ahead.

When you have a false confidence through routine, you may fall victim to becoming complacent as you believe that success will follow suit through routine. Routine becomes dangerous when it is predictable and boring. If you are predictable and have a tendency to become bored, then the routine has created complacency for you in your life. If it has happened in your business then this can create an avalanche of problems in your growth and performance. If your employees are going through mundane activities, day in, day out, with little change, then there is a high risk of this routine creating complacency.

As a business owner, you want to make sure your employees are always feeling slightly challenged and they are accomplishing tasks that are set out them. This helps them feel they are contributing meaningfully to the company and developing personally and professionally.

Making sure the staff are taken care of and that routine is not creating complacency within the business, should be a priority. You may like to introduce different schedules, tasks, or opportunities, to prevent any "boring tasks" and to make sure your employees remain on high alert.

While it's important to recognize and understand that even the most proficient professionals in their field will get stuck into a routine and are at risk of becoming complacent, by continually checking in and making sure that things are not done just because of routine, is an important key factor to making sure you are not at risk.

Hassan is sharing more in his INTERACTIVE book.

See exclusive videos, audios and photos.

DOWNLOAD it now at
deanpublishing.com/
whycomplacencykills

CASE STUDY

Have you ever considered that your morning routine is killing your creativity? Ironically, that hurried wake up routine is in fact the opposite conditions that neuroscientists and cognitive psychologists recommend stimulate creativity.

In a study published in the journal *Thinking and Reasoning*, researchers Mareike Wieth and Rose Zacks reported that our creativity and imaginative insights are most likely going to come to us when we're not focused.[5]

Why? Because it is in these moments where the mental processes that would originally inhibit thoughts are weak, and therefore allow creativity to flow.

Now go sip that morning coffee slowly!

---

5   Wieth, M., & Zacks, R. (2011). Time of day effects on problem solving: When the non-optimal is optimal. *Thinking & Reasoning*, 17(4),387401. https://doi.org/10.1080/13546783.2011.625663

CHAPTER 7

RESISTING CHANGE OR CHANGING RESISTANCE

Complacency results in the absence of change. When we introduce change, we eliminate the state of complacency. Human beings are "hardwired" to resist change. It is our human nature to resist change. Just as we are born as successful human beings, we have this internal resistance to change. Yet we often don't realize that change is constantly happening around us.

It takes a lot of mental energy and motivation to change our behavior or mentality. For example, trying to lose weight, or become fit and healthy. Any person wanting to achieve these goals will need to make significant changes to their physical lifestyle — what, when and how much they eat not to mention the essential physical exercise.

However, even when we know the strategies to follow to avoid obesity, lose weight or get healthy, making these changes is easier said than done. While we acknowledge that change is necessary, the problem is that our resistance to change can be so strong that we tend to resist it until we are faced with a crisis.

There are various reasons why we resist change.

FEAR OF THE UNKNOWN

Uncertainty about future events or situations often creates fear in people. How will the share market respond to a drop in interest rates? Will the market accept our new line of products? What if I don't like the job I am applying for? People usually only take action toward the unknown if they genuinely believe or feel that the risks of inaction are greater than those of taking action.

DENIAL OF THE NEED FOR CHANGE

Denial of the need for change is one of the main culprits for our resistance to it. Sure, the need for change might be evident, but if we're feeling comfortable and have "no reason" to change, then it's highly likely we won't change. Take for example, being overweight, where it's physically evident that something needs to change. Denying or ignoring this means we continue on the same path and risk our health.

ROUTINE AND COMFORT ZONE

As already outlined, routines make us feel safe, secure and comfortable. They eliminate the need for us to think hard or excessively to execute tasks. Changing our routines, like habits, requires hard work and can result in stress and anxiety.

Obviously, the idea of discomfort is unappealing, so we make excuses or resist the idea of the need to change.

IT AIN'T BROKEN

We've all heard the saying, "Why fix it if it ain't broken." Too often, this also becomes the mentality we also carry around. We tend to believe that the old ways of thinking, working or managing are good, because they're getting the job done. But "good" does not translate into "success" — and it comes with a lot of risk. So, while that rusty old water tap is still working, it might be contaminating our water at the same time. When we don't evaluate, assess and change our "old" ways of thinking then we run the risk of becoming outdated, obsolete or broken.

LIMITING BELIEFS AND SELF-ESTEEM

In previous chapters we have discussed the relationship between limiting beliefs and self-esteem in relation to contentment. It's also useful to look at this relationship and its effect on our ability to take action toward change.

Limiting beliefs are the biggest killer of positive thoughts and intended actions. When people don't believe they can competently manage change, there will likely be resistance. Our limiting beliefs do exactly that: they limit our belief that we are capable of change. They sabotage our own superior abilities to make changes.

THE STATUS QUO

Change may at times mean diverting from the status quo. It can mean doing things differently from everyone else. For many, diverting from the status quo represents a huge dilemma of "what if". The general concept is that the status quo is always "correct" or "right" — which means people fear that if they divert from the status quo they will be worse off.

Often this thinking is accompanied by the assumption that "if change was necessary, somebody would have done it already." A brilliant example of going against the status quo is when Apple introduced the first smart touch phone, the iPhone 3. It was a huge risk at a time, because trends in the market for phones were based on the need to be smaller and easily portable. The iPhone 3 was much larger than other phones. However, Apple took a gamble and it worked brilliantly, and they went on to create their own market.

CHANGING OUR RESISTANCE

Behavioral change is no simple matter. There is no magic pill or quick fix solution to changing the way we think or behave. But the good news is that we can change our mentality, thoughts, and personality if we choose to. We do that if we are passionate enough about the reason for change.

Our personalities and behaviors can change over time in direct relation to the effect of our environment. For change to occur in our thinking, behavior, and personality, we must want that change to occur with the utmost passion and desire. It is up to each person to make that decision within themselves to change or accept change.

The more we experience change, the more we become used to it and can adapt. If we look back at our lives and see some of the changes we've made — from moving jobs, changing careers, or moving countries — we can see how at first, it was difficult, but over time, we adjusted. And those changes have made us better versions of ourselves.

Complacency is the result of not making changes. Changes start in our thoughts and minds. With all things said, we can change our resistance to change. We can adjust our resistance to change to prevent complacency settling in. We are adaptable beings and change is part of being adaptable in our life. And remember, everything always turns out okay in the end, right?

CASE STUDY

Did you know that research by the *Journal of Clinical Psychology*, found that approximately 54% of people who commit to change fail to make the transformation last beyond six months?[6]

Many of us lack proper structures to support the behavioral changes our life goals require. The key to being able to make it happen depends on three things:

1. commitment
2. consistency
3. patience.

Use these principles as a guide, as you move through the changes you need to — and don't be afraid to reach out for support, if needed.

---

[6] Norcross, J. C., Mrykalo, M. S., & Blagys, M. D. (2002). Auld Lang Syne: Success predictors, change processes, and self-reported outcomes of New Year's resolvers and nonresolvers. *Journal of Clinical Psychology*, 58(4), 397–405. https://doi.org/10.1002/jclp.1151

> WE SHALL HAVE
> **NO BETTER CONDITIONS**
> IN THE FUTURE
> *– IF –*
> WE ARE **SATISFIED**
> WITH ALL THOSE WHICH
> WE HAVE AT PRESENT.
>
> — **THOMAS EDISON**

CHAPTER 8

OVATION FOR INNOVATION

In our modern society, great emphasis is placed on business leaders to introduce innovative practices and products into their business models. Innovation is nowadays regarded as the foundation of survival for enterprises and businesses alike. Our modern view is that innovation is understood to be technological and is often restricted to commercialized purposes.

Often however, when people think of innovation, they mistakenly associate (or confuse) this term, with improvisation and invention. I see it often, which is why it's important to get clear on these terms, before moving on.

Primarily, it is important that we extract a clear understanding about three words that would confuse almost anyone. These words are **improvisation, invention,** and **innovation.**

Innovation is a new idea or a way of doing something that has already been introduced or discovered. It's often seen as doing something better or offering a better solution to solve a problem. For example, motion sense garbage bins, or a smart oven.

It is not to be confused with improvisation (the act of doing something not planned, using whatever is available at the time. Like, being caught out in the rain and using the spare plastic bag you are carrying, as an umbrella) or invention, the process of creating something new (such as Artificial Intelligence (AI) machine learning, or Virtual Reality).

Did you know that the origin of the word "innovation" comes from the Latin *innovationem*, a noun of action from the word *innovare* which dates back to 1500 AD? The Middle Ages! In fact, at the peak of the Orthodox church, the reference of "innovator" given to someone was akin to charges of blasphemy or heresy. During those times, people who dared to express thoughts, ideas and suggestions that were contrary to the status quo, were termed innovators.

It's amazing when you think how far back this word stems and where it derived its meaning "to renew or change."[7] What is also useful to call out, is the origins of this word imply that innovation is more than just changing things, it's daring to go against the way things "have always been done."

Fast forward to the mid-1900s, and we see how companies and enterprises began to implement innovative practices in their services and products. It was no longer about inventing new products, but rather changing existing products or services.

---

7 Etymology Online Dictionary, (retrieved July 2020). https://www.etymonline.com/word/innovate

Innovation in enterprise became an essential element to market or sell products or services.

So how do we become "innovative"?

Innovation is a psychological behavior change.

Innovation is about changing human behavior and thinking. Real innovators would evaluate their communication skills to find a way to communicate better. They would assess the way they interact with society. They would analyze their own performance in fulfilling their duties or responsibilities. All this for one reason: to become a better and more efficient human being.

Having an innovative mind means that we are constantly looking and searching for better ways and methods to develop ourselves personally and professionally. Innovators are never content. They always tend to scrutinize the accuracy of their actions and results and are always searching for continuous improvement.

Bringing this to the business arena: when you hear the term "continuous improvement" you probably think of company quality assurance systems and processes. We have a perception that continuous improvement is a system that is applicable to companies or businesses only (and perhaps a little boring). For the sake of simplistic understanding, a continuous improvement plan (QIP) is a set of activities designed to bring gradual, ongoing improvement to products, services, or processes through constant review, measurement, and action. Organizations that are dedicated to their continuous improvement policy understand the importance of these policies for strengthening the quality of a product, improving customer satisfaction, and improving efficiency, productivity and profits. Often, QIPs form part of the basic operational system of an organization.

Having continuous improvement systems and policies in organizations is an excellent way of ensuring that the products and services are regularly reviewed and either improved or replaced by better ones. Continuous improvement systems have become an essential element of survival for businesses and organizations. This is where innovation steps in, because an effective continuous improvement plan, requires innovation.

These types of continuous improvement systems are not just relatable to a business. In fact, we can apply these concepts to any area of our life: personal, family, finances, career.

Having a continuous improvement plan, means you become the innovator of you entire life. You become the brains, the ideas, and the creation behind radical improvements in your life!

Which means that complacency would not get a look in: we've become innovative in our thoughts, our perceptions and subsequently, in our attitudes and our physical practices, routines, work, products and social behavior are positively impacted.

FIVE STEPS TO KICKING OFF A CONTINUOUS IMPROVEMENT PROGRAM

STEP 1
Get your management team onboard. Support and encouragement from an organization's leadership team is a critical success factor of a continuous improvement initiative.

STEP 2
Start small. If you are new to change or continuous improvement, then starting small is best. Many businesses

have seen success by starting with smaller-scale projects before moving into bigger changes.

STEP 3
Get your employees involved. Your teams are going to make or break the success of any continuous improvement initiative. Get them on board form the outset. Their ideas and valuable.

STEP 4
Get comfortable with making mistakes. You might not get things right on the first try every time, which is okay. Make it safe to fail and try new ways of making things work.

STEP 5
Communicate the difference. Continuous improvement often requires small, incremental changes — rather than massive overhauls. Commit progress allows your employees to feel part of the change and process.

Our world is constantly evolving. In turn, we must evolve too, in our behavior. In contrast to the fifteenth century, the innovators of our time are the heroes of our modern world. We need to innovate how we think and communicate. We need to innovate how we work and interact. We need to innovate how we learn and practice. We need to innovate how to live and survive. It all starts within you.

> **OUR GOALS** CAN ONLY BE **REACHED** THROUGH THE VEHICLE OF A PLAN.
>
> THERE IS **NO OTHER ROUTE** TO SUCCESS.
>
> — PABLO PICASSO

CHAPTER 9
COMMUNICATION IS THE KEY

Communication in business spans many areas. From internal upward or downward communication with managers and employees, to lateral communication with colleagues, to external communications with customers, communication is critical.

However, many people underestimate the power of communication and do not realize that it is a crucial element to building, sustaining and having a successful business. It is also intrinsically linked to complacency, which is what this chapter will explore.

Communication is important on every level so that your clients, customers, employees and anyone seeking your services is not confused. The latter is especially important, as you risk losing prospects and business. I have seen business owners fall into the trap where they become complacent and comfortable, in turn letting communication slip.

There are many ways we communicate. For you to ensure you are communicating effectively — internally and externally — it is important to understand the different types and styles.

There are three main types of communication: verbal (sound and language); non-verbal (body language and expressions); and visual (anything you can see).

VERBAL COMMUNICATION

This form of communication is what most people are familiar with and includes tone, language, and speech. Verbal communication makes up 41% of our communication: 7% words and 34% tone.[8]

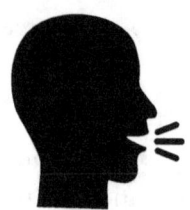

Verbal communication also includes emotional intelligence, which is our ability to understand and manage emotions, including those of the people around us. Being aware of how emotions may be filtering through in your language and speech by paying attention to your tone, the language you are using (whether it is positive or negative) and how you are perceived, is very important.

When we do not get verbal communicate right, we place ourselves and our business at risk. Think miscommunication, arguments, friction; these things we want to avoid.

A useful exercise to understand how you're using language and tone is to have someone record you when you are running

---

[8] Thomson, Jeff Dr. (Sep 30, 2011) Beyond Words Blog, "Is Nonverbal Communication a Numbers Game?" *Psychology Today*. https://www.psychologytoday.com/au/blog/beyond-words/201109/is-nonverbal-communication-numbers-game

a meeting or taking a seminar. This will give you the means to listen to your communication and how it is coming across to others. You may find that you use a lot of negative words or that you take too many pauses. Or, you may find that you sound too passive, or too aggressive. Or it may be perfect! Take the time to find your perfect verbal communication style and where needed, some training to support you.

NON-VERBAL

Non-verbal communication — and the importance of this — is often overlooked. This type of communication includes body language, facial expressions and even things that you are not saying. This type of communication can really help identify important clues to a person's thoughts and feelings.

Just like our verbal communication, we want to avoid risk. For example, avoiding rolling your eyes at a colleagues suggestions or comments as it appears rude. Or avoiding slamming papers on the desk as this comes across as aggressive.

As a business leader, you want to be showing a confident and approachable non-verbal communication style which is also welcoming and open to new ideas so it allows your staff — and clients — to feel safe.

VISUAL COMMUNICATION

This type of communication refers to any non-verbal communication that uses sight. It also includes how you dress, how you sit and even how you choose to

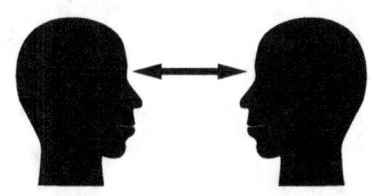

walk. Because this type of communication is visual, it's incredibly powerful.

Think about what you see every moment of every day, and what messages are being communicated to you. For example, if you were in the workplace wearing a suit, and someone arrived wearing ripped jeans and an old t-shirt, what would you think? Or, what about seeing a colleague leaning back in their chair, or slouching in front of the computer?

These types of situations speak volumes about how a person is thinking or feelings. People who feel sad will most likely be slouching, people who are shy will almost always be covering their body somehow, or their face. A confident person will walk with their back straight, hair out of their face, shoulders back, and a smile on their face, with a welcoming approach to life.

Visual communication also portends to your surroundings in your office and your reception space. What is the first thing your staff or clients see when they walk into your office? Is it clutter? Is it negative imagery? Is it positive? What message are you trying to convey and is it clear? What is the attitude you are communicating to people visually?

Like verbal and non-verbal communication, getting this right, is also critically important.

TOP TIPS FOR HOW TO FAIL PROOF YOUR COMMUNICATION

Knowing is one thing, acting is another — which is why I have listed some top tips on how to improve communications, avoid mishaps — and complacency.

TIP 1

Listen

Listening seems to be an easy task, but many people go through their day and forget the majority of what happened. This is because they did not  partake in active listening. Active listening is a skill you can acquire, with practice. Active listening is when you stop, make full eye contact, give that person your full attention (no multi-tasking here) and do not interrupt. No talking, just purely listening.

When we're more cognizant to listening, we may in fact find in our own behavior, that we speak over people to get a point across. If this is you, that's okay, just make sure you recognize when you need to take time to engage in active listening and step back from the talking. If you can practice this regularly, you will find that your memory of conversations and the day will improve, and you will have a higher retention rate with clients. They will feel heard and appreciated and you will have a great communication style. Learn to listen!

"I believe a good leader brings out the best in people by listening to them, trusting in them, believing in them, respecting them and letting them have a go."
Richard Branson

TIP 2

Choose your words carefully

Words are powerful; and while only 7% of our verbal communication, they hold weight. Often, we speak without thinking — and have  all been guilty of saying things that we regret, or if given the chance, would rephrase or choose different words.

Taking the time to pause momently before speaking, gives enough time for you to hear the message and choose the right words before responding. And when we're engaged in active listening and present in the conversation we're even better equipped to choose the best response.

It might seem small, but choosing words deliberately and with intent, is powerful. So think before speaking!

All great leaders and orators are masters of language and carefully consider the words they use, knowing that words can be weapons, words can heal and words can transform. They choose them carefully.

"Be careful with your words. Once they are said, they can only be forgiven not forgotten."
Unknown

TIP 3

Monitor your tone and body language

When we speak, sometimes our emotions can show through our tone. Being conscious about how we feel and dealing with that before entering anything  that is of relevance in business, is important.

For example, making sure that you are calm before entering any important meeting, so that your tone does not reflect negatively.

There are some great hacks for getting your body language in place. One great way is through visualization, deep breathing and rolling your shoulders back. You want to communicate that you are ready, on task and willing to take on the job, rather than appearing passive, shy or angry. One of my favorites is to check yourself in front of a mirror.

If you do not have access to a mirror, you can also do this by being aware of your body. Is your body slouching? Are your shoulders hunched forward? Are you frowning? Is your jaw clenched? Are you making a fist? Do your muscles feel tight? How do your shoulders feel?

Feel your body and see how you are feeling. This can be done in a few moments at any time of the day.

TIP 4

Only give what is needed

Many people will give unwanted or unnecessary advice to people because they think that the other person is
doing it "wrong". If you are the type of person who is continually giving out advice, even when not asked, then this may come across as arrogant and standoffish. In fact, if we take a step back, we may be surprised to learn another way to do something. This one goes hand-in-hand with Tip 1.

Unwarranted or unsolicited advice may be well-meaning and with good intentions, however if that person didn't ask for your advice, then giving it without an invitation is usually met with some apprehension from the one on the receiving end.

Only give what is needed.

Learn to listen to the people around you, and then jump in when you know it can be of value to them or the conversation. Remember that a conversation involves two parties or more and it's important that everybody feels valued, heard and seen. Bombarding people with advice isn't the best strategy to develop long-term relationships and build rapport.

TIP 5

Reassess your wardrobe and office surroundings

Self-explanatory, but important.

If you have been wearing the same shoes for the past 7 years and they are scraped and falling apart at the seams, then you are showing potential  clients and your staff that they are not worthy of a well presented person. And you are also communicating to yourself that you are not worthy, by failing to buy a pair of new shoes! In these situations, it might be useful to ask the question: "If I were to hire me, would I consider myself?" or "What do I need to change visually to make myself appear caring and confident?" or "What can I wear that makes me feel good and gives me confidence?"

Do the same thing in your office. Walk in with fresh eyes and see what needs to be cleaned up, thrown away, recycled or changed. It might be as simple as putting up a new piece of art, or buying a couple of pot plants, or adding your favorite photos or quotes to your office wall to keep you refreshed and inspired. You can also add some invigorating scents to your workplace by burning candles or using diffusers.

Taking the time to check ourselves, and our surroundings is a useful way to recognize what we need to adjust, to be our best selves.

Every employer should have a great communication style and be continually learning. While the tips above are a great foundation, take time to update your skills, enrol in personal development courses or learn how to manage conflicts so you're operating at your best.

CHAPTER 10
MOTIVATION VERSUS INSPIRATION

Often, many people confuse the term "inspiration" with "motivation".

Living in our modern world I grew up hearing the term motivation and how important it is to get or stay motivated to achieve success or fulfill our goals. In fact, if we look around the world, we can see that the word "motivation" has become one of the most used word by leading figures (e.g. coaches) to drive others to achieve their goals.

Well, news flash: I believe that motivation is bad for you.

Let me explain.

Motivation is not what we need to be successful in life.

I know you may be shocked to read this; in fact, I was shocked when I discovered this too. To help explain the why, it is first important to understand what motivation is.

The word "motivation" is derived from the word "motive" which means the needs, desires or wants of an individual, that causes a person to act.

Motivation then, can be considered influenced by the external; when something or someone compels, instructs or even forces you to take action. These motivators can be positive or negative. For example, we may be motivated by hitting a sales target which translates into more money for us. Or, we may be motivated to meet a looming deadline, because you know that your boss, or client is so fierce, you want to avoid the wrath.

Inspiration on the hand, is something that we feel inside, that encourages us to take action. The feelings we experience when we reach a point of willingness to act; the inner drive that keeps us moving.

While in any business there will be varying degrees and needs for both inspiration and motivation, it's being able to separate the two that is critical. The important differentiation between the two, is when we look at how they work in practice.

When we try to motivate people by using incentives, we focus on using external — which means we get people to act, change or behave in response to something, not because of a true cause. For example, offering your employees a raise if they sell more products. On face value this might appear fine, but if you're only motivating people by money alone — including those who might be underperforming — the incentive isn't going to last very long. Sure, you might get a few more sales, but you'll still have underperforming people!

When someone is acting from a space of inspiration, they do things because they want to. When you are inspired, you naturally do things you want, or need to, rather than doing it for someone or something else. You act willingly and happily.

Inspiration is a driving force, whereas motivation is a pulling force. To use an analogy, consider a fire. Motivation is the sticks you throw on a fire to keep it burning, while inspiration is the fire itself.

I'm sure there have been times in your life where you've felt both motivated and inspired. Think about how you felt. Is it clear to you now that there is a difference?

Now that we have clarified the difference between motivation and inspiration, we can talk about the link between inspiration and complacency.

In simple terms, if you are not inspired then you lose ambition and drive and become complacent.

Let me share with you my personal story.

Growing up, I had a dilemma of feeling like I had "two lives". On the one hand, I had my mother adoring and spoiling me in every way, while on the other, my opinion and thoughts were disregarded as I was the youngest child. As a result, I grew up with the mentality that my opinion was not good enough for anyone. I grew up thinking that I was not smart enough to contribute to family matters. I grew up thinking I was not intelligent, but rather just a person who would follow instructions and obey orders.

At an early stage of my life, I stopped contributing ideas and thoughts to other people for two reasons. The first was the fear that my opinions and ideas would be rejected and second, my belief that my thinking or opinion was not good enough for anyone.

Often, when your opinion is not regarded well within your immediate family, then it has a domino effect and flows on to the external social arena. And for me, this is what happened. I was psychologically affected.

Not feeling good enough or recognized, forced me into a position where I felt a need to prove myself — alongside the word "no" being unacceptable. A desire started to grow inside me to show to the whole world who I was. I wanted to prove to my family that I was not the "baby" brother that they always knew and that I was smarter and more capable than what they had always believed about me.

With my passion for airplanes, I decided to become a pilot. As I knew it would be financially difficult, I opted to join the air force to make that happen. However, my application was rejected on the basis that I had not been in Australia for more than 10 years at that time. The answer was a resounding, "no".

I did not give up. Thinking of an alternative pathway, I was accepted into RMIT to undertake a degree in Aerospace Engineering. While being denied an opportunity to work with Boeing as it was based in the US, and Malaysia Airlines in Kuala Lumpur for practical training, I continued to move forward. When I graduated, my first job as an Aerospace Engineer, was for the Department of Defense and subsequently for the Royal Australian Air Force (RAAF). I had made it!

Sure, I was motivated to achieve, to show my family who I had become, but it was my passion for the air force that drove me. My why, fueled my inspiration.

We have all heard the term "where there's a will there's a way". If you want something so strongly, so passionately and with such belief, it will become your will to find a way to make it happen. Not only do you have the power to make it happen, you have the power to make it happen your way. The way you want it.

At times in our lives, events, circumstances and situations do not flow in the way that we desire. But opportunities will come to those who believe.

Need an inspiration pick me up? Here are my top five tips for helping re-invigorate the inspiration wheel (or keep it running) — and avoid becoming complacent.

1. Define or revisit your values
2. Try something new
3. Take on a challenge
4. Be open to change
5. Don't take "no" for an answer!

TIP 1

Define or revisit your values

whether personal or business. Often when we are going through the motions of life, we forget about the "why" — instead, looking at the "what". To gain inspiration, it is important to connect with your values, and your why. Ask yourself why you, or your business, are doing X, Y, or Z. It can be quite a tough question, so if you don't know the answers that's okay — it gives you a great opportunity to find out!

TIP 2

Try something new

As we have already touched on before, getting stuck in routine is easy, which sometimes reduces our inspiration because we get stuck in the same patterns. Trying or learning something new is a great way to reinvigorate this spark and even find something new that inspires you. It could be finally taking the team out for lunch once a month, enrolling yourself in a professional development course, or changing your business strategy.

TIP 3

Take on a challenge

Sometimes we are prone to limiting ourselves; in fact, a lot of us fall victim to fear. Don't let fear cripple you or stop you from living your dreams. Taking on a new challenge is a great way of shaking things up — and gives you the option of potentially finding something to sink your teeth into.

If you are a business, go pitch to that client you have been putting off, restructure your business, or set new incredible targets to achieve success!

TIP 4

Be open to change

If you have found your business is suffering from a lack of inspiration and innovation, it is time for change. Sure, it might not be clear what that change might be, or how it will work, but taking the time to assess your business, as it is, is a great way to find any gaps, weakness or areas for improvement. You can always engage an experienced business coach to help you elevate your business to the next level.

TIP 5

Don't take "no" for an answer!

The word "no" is not a wall. The word "no" is not an obstacle. It is merely a challenge to overcome. Don't run from the word "no" if somebody says that to you, it is merely a word you can use now to find another route, another way, until you hear a YES! "No" can drive you to accomplish things you never thought possible.

"Persist – don't take no for an answer. If you're happy to sit at your desk and not take any risk, you'll be sitting at your desk for the next 20 years."
David Rubenstein

> **WISE MEN**
> TALK BECAUSE THEY HAVE SOMETHING TO SAY;
>
> **FOOLS,**
> BECAUSE THEY HAVE TO SAY SOMETHING.
>
> — PLATO

CHAPTER 11

ARE YOU LIVING ON AUTOPILOT?

Over the years, life has become more comfortable, easier, and convenient — at least for most of us. We live in a privileged era of technological advancements, where new systems, tools and processes continue to make our lives more comfortable. In fact, some of us seek these opportunities out; testing the boundaries, seeking the "new", to find ways to do things better. We live in a society where evolution is paramount.

Our knowledge is infinite — and so too is the technology journey the world is on. We only need to look around the world to seek the rapid rate of technological advancements over the years. The release of the internet in early 1990s, was one of the biggest turning points — introducing the world to the "world wide web" of data and information. As a result, it has become extremely easy to get access to relevant information and data at anytime and anywhere.

Another essential element that has been simplified through technology is communication. Modern technology such as email systems, video conferencing, Short Message Service (SMS) and social media platforms have simplified our inter-personal and our inter-national, communications to an extent where our communications is transferred to any part of the world, in a matter of seconds.

But the one technological revolution that fascinates me the most is the evolution of transportation systems. Transportation technology is evolving at an exponential rate. The level of technology that we see and experience nowadays in modern transportation vehicles such as cars, trains and planes is almost beyond comprehension. Modern transportation technology has made it easy to travel long distances over a shorter period — and will only continue to increase. While these advancements have been of huge value, there is always the other side of the coin. We use technologies in many ways and sometimes the way we implement various technologies into our lives can do more harm than good.

While working with Boeing commercial airplanes, I was always amazed by the autopilot function on commercial airplanes. Autopilot is an electronic system on airplanes that is used to control or maintain the designated flight path of an aircraft, without the need for constant hands-on control or input by a human operator (pilot). The autopilot system can instantly respond to air pockets or "turbulent conditions" during the flight, but it can't fly the plane all the way or land without the direction of the pilot.

With all its benefits, the autopilot has a dangerous side. The dangerous side of this autopilot system, is that if the human operator (pilot) becomes incapacitated, disabled or unwilling to provide input for a long period of time, the plane will continue to fly in the same pattern, at the same altitude. Eventually, it will run out of fuel or fly into adversities.

So, why is this relevant?

Believe it or not, humans also have a built-in "autopilot". Our autopilot is a self-activating mechanism controlled by our brain. It switches itself on and off automatically without us realizing. To give a clearer understanding on how our "autopilot" is activated or deactivated, let's take a look at how "autopilot" works.

At birth, our brain has over 100 billion inter-connectable brain cells, called neurons. Our bodily functions are controlled by these neurons. The neuron is the basic working unit of the brain. The neuron is designed to transmit information to other neurons, muscles, or gland cells. Think of a neuron as a tree with three main parts: the dendrites, an axon, and a cell body. A dendrite, represented as a tree branch, is where a neuron receives input from other cells. Dendrites branch as they move towards their tips, just like tree branches do.

The axon, represented as a tree root, is the output structure of the neuron. In simple terms, when a neuron wants to talk to another neuron, it sends an electrical message called an action potential throughout the entire axon. At the end of each tip is a connectable called synapses which connect to other neuron dendrites. The cell body, represented as a tree trunk, is where the nucleus of the neuron is. The cell body is the "central brain" of the neuron.

Dendrites pick up chemical signals across a synapse and the impulse travels the length of the axon. Connection between two neurons is initiated when the synapses of neuron (A) connects to the dendrites of neuron (B).

When we do a task for the first time, this connection is initiated between neuron (A) and neuron (B). Now if we repeat this same routine task on a regular basis, then this connection between neuron (A) and neuron (B) is consistently and repeatedly activated. Thus, making this connection a strong — and possibly permanent — connection.

Over time, the neurons memorize the sequential firings that need to take place between neurons for this task to be completed. In other words, the brain starts an unconscious decision-making system (the "autopilot") so it can take care of routine tasks without exerting energy. The neurons switch into "autopilot" mode and transmit the required and relevant messages to one another. This "autopilot" can actually serve us well at times — because our brain cannot possibly take the time to process every single thing and action we do. Our brain switches itself on "autopilot" on the most repeated tasks and activities that we do in our normal lives.

Scientifically, it is said that we make about 35,000 decisions every day. From simple decisions such as what to wear, or what to eat, to more complex decisions. Our ability to think, analyze and reason at any given moment is a cognitive functionality of our brain. To conserve energy, our brain will kick into "autopilot" to allow our conscious mind to work on other more complex matters.

Operating on autopilot takes two forms:
1. Small scale autopilot: this is an automatic, fast, and unconscious way of thinking. For example, our day to day routine activities such as driving to work, preparing a meal, what shoes, or dress to wear. This small scale autopilot is autonomous and efficient but very deceptive, as it is highly prone to bias and repetitive errors.

2. Large scale autopilot: sharing the same principles of small scale autopilot, it tends to play out in the larger elements of life. For example, our relationships, careers and financial matters.

The amount of times over the years, that I would arrive at home or at work and realize I couldn't remember stopping at any traffic lights, changing lanes or making any right-hand or left hand turns, has been countless. I am sure most of you can relate to this experience, where small scale autopilot is in control.

On a larger scale, autopilot has had a more dramatic impact on my life. Securing my first job with Boeing Commercial Airplanes, was an ultimate dream come true for me at that time. Being newly married with a young son and working my dream 9 to 5 job seemed like a perfect life.

Perfect enough, that it slipped into autopilot. My Monday to Friday routine was so ingrained, I became a machine. With that, no ambitions, or dreams outside of the job existed. I lacked lust for life and inspiration to become something bigger than an ordinary employee. I had basically entered a stagnant period of complacency.

If I had of recognized that just like that airplane, operating on autopilot would result in a crash — losing motivation, money, and direction — I'd have taken the hint earlier on.

After the first year in my job, I had no money left from my salary. I thought that the year ahead would be different, however, I continued being complacent and continued in autopilot for the second year. Nothing changed; I finished that year still trying to make ends meet.

Unfortunately, most people operate on "autopilot" in everyday life. Without the direct input, planning and influence necessary to change, many people subsequently run out of "fuel". In autopilot mode, we tend to respond to eventuated circumstances, events and situations as they happen, rather than being in control of designing our future. We just let our future happen, as our brain ends up making decisions for us — decisions that may not be the best decisions! Our response to challenging situations is often defensive, condemnation of oneself, or condemnation of others or simply finding excuses, because we resist to see our own part in the disaster.

Living in "autopilot" is a core indication of complacency.

The good news is, we can decide whether we want to be operating in autopilot. Just like the airplane, we can choose to flick that switch off, take control and divert our flight path from complacency and back to the correct route.

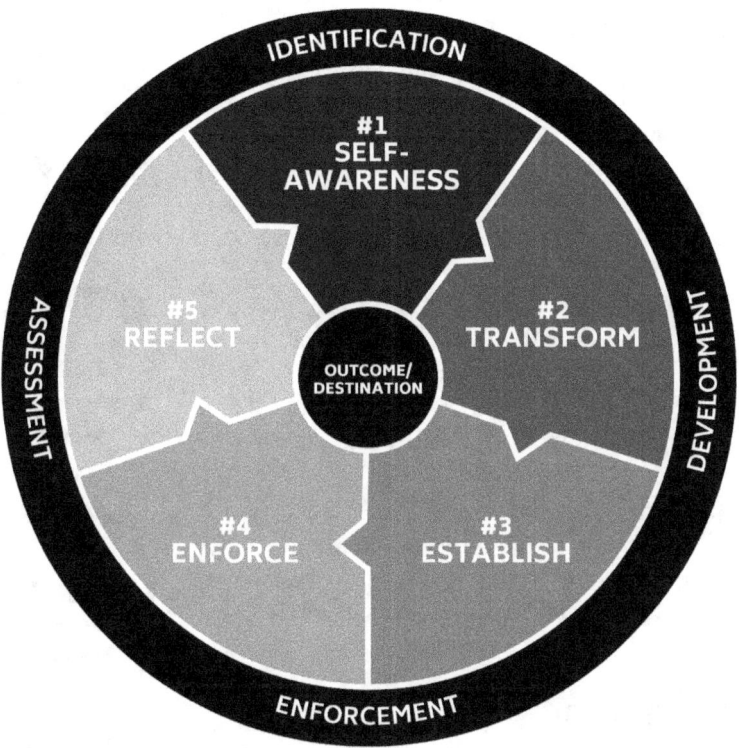

I   **IDENTIFICATION PHASE**
Identification of strengths, weaknesses, values, traits, skills and abilities through self-awareness.

D   **DEVELOPMENT PHASE**
Development of skills, true values. True vision, goals, objectives to achieve transformation.

E   **ENFORCEMENT PHASE**
Enforcement of action plan based on the vision, mission and objectives.

A   **ASSESSMENT PHASE**
Assess the entire process through reflection and valuation of outcome achievement.

S SELF-AWARENESS

Increase your self-awareness by becoming more aware your own behavior and attitude. Ask yourself, are you making your own choices or letting your autopilot choose for you?

T TRANSFORM

Transform yourself or your business. Transformation can and should occur after becoming self-aware. This allows you to consciously transform yourself and your business with clarity and purpose.

E ESTABLISH

Establish your true values, your inner vision (inspiration) and your personal and business mission, and goals. Establish your culture and environment.

E ENFORCE

Enforce your true vision, mission, objectives, goals and culture. They are all wonderful to have outlined, but they remain useless until they are implemented and enforced.

R REFLECT

Reflect on the outcomes and performance. Reflect on practices and processes and notice the best areas for improvement and adjustment. Reflection is another word for reviewing. You can repeat this cycle every 3 to 6 months. It is easy to fall into old habits if you are not continuously reviewing and reflecting upon your actions. Repeating the steps and reviewing where you're at, will keep you in check.

STEER YOURSELF IN THE RIGHT DIRECTION

Just like it is easy to deploy the autopilot system on a plane, it is extremely easy for our brain to put our lives into "autopilot". I've been there, you've been there, and a lot of people are still operating on that level right now. Make a decision to flick the autopilot switch off, switch gears and take control.

STEER can be used for any type of scenario: business, personal, financial. health and well-being, leadership, career pathways etc.

The simplest approach to avoid going into autopilot is to STEER yourself in the right direction. Yes, you heard me! The STEER strategy is a simple, effective way to introduce ideas, methods and practices, that will disrupt your "autopilot" thoughts and kick you in to action. Steering means that you take hold of the direction and don't allow autopilot to be your default state.

You will notice that it's not only about brainstorming and reflection, it's also about enforcing your goals and desires, ensuring that you bring them into action. Nothing moves until you take action.

It's important to create your own personal STEER strategy, because no one should be steering your life's direction, except YOU. If you don't hold the steering wheel of your life, it's means that someone else is.

> *"You are the architect of your own destiny; you are the master of your own fate; you are behind the steering wheel of your life. There are no limitations to what you can do, have, or be. Accept the limitations you place on yourself by your own thinking."*
> **Brian Tracy**

YOUR PERSONAL STEER STRATEGY
S – SELF AWARENESS

Are you making your own choices or letting your autopilot choose for you? What are some choices you can consciously make today?

....

....

....

....

....

....

....

....

....

....

....

....

....

T – TRANSFORM

What areas of your business or life do you want to transform and why?

E – ESTABLISH

Take time to establish your true values, your inner vision (inspiration) and your personal and business mission, and goals. Establish your culture and environment.

My Values:

....

....

....

....

....

....

....

....

....

....

....

....

My Inner Vision:

Personal Mission:

Business Mission:

Personal Goals:

Business Goals:

Personal Culture:

Business Culture:

Personal Environment:

Business Environment:

E – ENFORCE

How will you enforce your true vision, mission, objectives, goals and culture? What steps will you take you ensure they stay a primary focus?

Ways I Will Enforce My Values:

....

....

....

....

....

....

....

....

....

....

....

....

....

....

Ways I Will Enforce My Inner Vision:

Ways I Will Enforce My Personal Mission:

Ways I Will Enforce My Business Mission:

Ways I Will Enforce My Personal Goals:

Ways I Will Enforce My Business Goals:

Ways I Will Enforce My Personal Culture:

Ways I Will Enforce My Business Culture:

Ways I Will Enforce My Personal Environment:

Ways I Will Enforce My Business Environment:

....

....

....

....

....

....

....

....

....

....

Hassan is sharing more in his INTERACTIVE book.

See exclusive videos, audios and photos.

DOWNLOAD it now at **deanpublishing.com/ whycomplacencykills**

R – REFLECT

Reflect on the outcomes and performance. Reflect on practices and processes and notice the best areas for improvement and adjustment. Write your reflections down and consider areas to adjust or adapt.

....

....

....

....

....

....

....

....

....

....

....

....

....

....

....

....

....

ARE YOU LIVING ON AUTOPILOT?

> **EVERYTHING**
> THAT YOU HAVE WORKED SO
> HARD TO ACHIEVE MAY DISAPPEAR
> — **IF YOU** —
> **BECOME COMPLACENT.**
>
> — HASSAN YOUNES

CHAPTER 12

MIND YOUR COMPANY

Breaking news: The people you spend the most time with shape who you are.

Why? Influence.

It is a fact that the people we surround ourselves with have the biggest influence on our behavior, attitudes, and results. The dictionary definition of influence explains it as the people or situations that affect what we do, or how we act. What it does not identify however, is the types of influence which can be positive, negative, or even neutral.

In our society we talk generally about the negative and positive influence of people on each other. It is often easy to identify where positive influences are in our life; from the mentor you have found in a new connection, to your morning meditations, or the worldly podcasts you listen to. Similarly, we can also identify where negative influences may be occurring: the friend who is constantly criticizing your work, the amount of alcohol that you consume each day to the two-hour travel commute to work and back.

However, we tend to ignore the neutral influence that people have on us. Which unfortunately, is as bad as negative influence.

So, what do we mean when we talk about neutral influence? On face value, the term "neutral" implies just that: impartial, unbiased, indifferent. The hidden issue with this term is that it implies no impact — which is incorrect.

A person of neutral influence is someone who does not express their opinion, feedback, ideas or suggestions — and always agree with others. Their reasons for doing so, are often founded on the basis of various personal or behavioral reasons.

Growing up, I had a friend who fit the "neutral type". He never gave ideas or suggestions and would always agree on any opinion or ideas that I had. He never expressed his thoughts on anything we did — remaining quiet most of the time we played together. It felt like he was a tag along friend and any time spent playing with him felt stale. Because of this, I started to resent spending time with him, so ended up slowly distancing myself.

I think you would agree that it is annoying when you are with someone who gives a neutral stance on every suggestion or opinion. Having to be that person who always makes suggestions, or decisions — because if not, nothing would happen, and you would both end up nowhere! Neutral people are the type who are scared to give opinions for fear of incorrectness or a negative outcome. Neutral people are content in where and how they stand. These people are complacent people.

Now we know that mixing with a type of person will have an influence on you, so it is essential to avoid being associated with negative people as well as neutral people. These types of people will have a detrimental effect on you and lead you down the path of complacency.

In simple words, dump your "friends" who fit the above. Yes, this advice might sound rather harsh and insensitive but the reality is, if you don't change your company, they'll change you.

Out with the old, in with the new.

TOP 4 STEPS
STEPS TO HELP YOU IDENTIFY WHO STAYS AND WHO GOES

STEP 1

Spend some time thinking about the five people you spend most of your time with. When you think about these five people, is that where you see yourself? Is that where you want to be? Are these people growing and challenging you to grow? Are they living the life that you want for yourself, for your family and for whatever you want your career to be? What type of influence are they having on your life?

STEP 2

Give yourself permission to let people go. If you look at these five people and realize they're balancing the influence scales in the opposite direction — and they may not be for you — you need to make that tough decision. I get it. It was a tough decision for me and it drew negative responses from people (which is normal). But like me, you can make the decision to minimize the amount of time you spend with these people — and put yourself first.

STEP 3

Make room for positive influence in your life. Seek new friends who are more successful or qualified than you are. New friends who are more experienced and confident in what they do. Seek new friends who can inspire you to grow, who can challenge you to become a better person and who live the life that you want to have. The key to this friendship quest is to expand your social connections through networking events,

social media platforms and people connections. Seek out and attend new events such as training seminars and conferences. Set yourself a target of valuable friends that will help you towards your dreams.

STEP 4

Get a coach if you need to. Most of the challenges that we face are based on our limiting beliefs and fear. A mentor or coach will challenge your thinking and beliefs and then draw out your confidence to achieve what you thought you could not.

No man is an island. We all need support from others to move on, strive or survive. Sir Richard Branson once said, "Surround yourself with people who bring out the best in you." Do this. Surround yourself with people who bring out the best in you. From friends to colleagues, to mentors or coaches, you have the resources available to surround yourself with positive people.

CASE STUDY

Renowned businessman Jim Rohn once said, "You are the average of the five people you spend most of your time with" — and he's right. In fact, a study completed by Binghamton University, New York has demonstrated the impacts of influence on success, in school children.

The study examined the correlation between the social positions of Kindergarten to year 12 students and how this impacted behavior and academic achievements. The methodology had students divide into one of five groups (best friends, friends, acquaintances, strangers, or relatives) where academic performance was monitored across that year. The correlation most significant, was at the friendship level. In fact, students whose friends outperformed them in school were more likely to improve their own test scores, while students whose friends had lower grades were more likely to have declining test scores.[9]

---

9   Blansky D, Kavanaugh C, Boothroyd C, Benson B, Gallagher J, Endress J, et al. (February 13, 2013) Spread of Academic Success in a High School Social Network. *PLoS ONE* 8(2): e55944. https://doi.org/10.1371/journal.pone.0055944

> IT'S NOT A VERY BIG STEP FROM **CONTENTMENT** TO **COMPLACENCY.**
>
> — SIMONE DE BEAUVOIR

> I THINK IT'S **DANGEROUS** TO THINK THAT YOU'RE SUCCESSFUL, — BECAUSE THEN — **YOU BECOME COMPLACENT.**
>
> — TOMMY HILFIGER

CHAPTER 13
INTERNAL LAWS OF PHYSICS

While studying physics during high school, I was introduced to Newton's laws of motion. Newton's laws of motion consist of three laws that, together, form the basis of many analytical and mathematical solutions in the world of physics and science.

Now, you might be wondering why I am talking about Newton in a book on complacency. Well there is a point: in fact, an important one — in that the laws of motion and complacency are in fact, linked.

To understand how, let's take a look at each, one by one.

LAW #1

Newton's first law of motion states that an object at rest will stay at rest, and an object in motion will stay in motion with the same speed and move in the same direction unless acted upon by an external force. This is also referred to as inertia.

Newton's first law of motion predicts the behavior of objects for which all existing forces are balanced. The first law states that if the forces acting upon an object are balanced in all directions, then the acceleration of that object in any direction will be nil. Objects at equilibrium (the condition in which all forces balance) will not move or accelerate in any direction. A great example of this is a dining table. The dining table will remain in its state of rest, in a state of equilibrium, because the weight acting downward is balanced by the same upward force from the floor. According to Newton, an object will only accelerate if there is a net or unbalanced force acting upon it. The presence of balanced forces will not accelerate an object — nor change its speed, direction, or both. So, the dining table will not move until a person exerts a small horizontal force on the dining table, enough to overcome the floor friction. If we take that and apply it to an object's motion, the same principles apply.

Let's look at an air hockey game table. The air hockey table has many tiny holes on its surface where a small flow of air is coming out. The puck sits on the table surface in mid-air due to the force of the air pushing it up. In this state, the puck is in a state of equilibrium as the downward force (weight) is balanced by upward force (air).

When the puck is hit horizontally, a net (external horizontal force) is exerted onto it, which causes the puck to move in the same direction as the force. The puck keeps moving forward until it's either (a) acted upon by an external force (for example, hitting the edge of the table and bouncing off) or (b) slowing down due to the air resistance acting in the opposite direction of its movement.

Now, it is the natural tendency of physical objects to resist changes in their state of motion. This tendency to resist changes in their state of motion is where the principle of inertia steps in. If we use an example, think about what happens when you're traveling on a train, or in a car, and it suddenly comes to a stop. Our body's physical inertia tends to resist this change in forward speed, and we jerk forward

In the same way, we also have, what I like to call, "mental inertia". That is we all have the tendency to resist change in any situation or circumstance until we are acted upon by an external set of events or circumstances that forces us to make changes to our thinking and behavior. The type of "external force" we expose ourselves to, is usually up to us. Our family members, our friends, our colleagues and peers, business associates and our coaches are all external forces that may have a direct impact on our direction or state of equilibrium (stagnation) in life. Other external forces may be the state of the economy, the competition, health and fitness or even culture and limiting beliefs.

By understanding this first law, we can predict our behavior and minimize the risk of complacency in our lives.

"You have to make the rules, not follow them."
Isaac Newton

LAW #2

Newton's second law of motion is a quantitative description of the changes that a force can produce on the motion of an object. It is summed up in the equation F (force) = M (mass) x A (acceleration). Basically, it states that the acceleration of an object is dependent upon two variables: the net force acting upon the object and the mass of the object.

An example, let's look at two identical trucks (truck A and truck B) having the same engine capacity, traveling on the same stretch of road in similar conditions. Truck A is fully loaded and heavy. Truck B is not loaded and therefore lighter than truck A. Now truck A, due to its heavy load will require far more engine power, torque and fuel to accelerate to a speed of 60 km/hr. Truck B will require much less engine power and torque to accelerate to the same speed of 60km/hr.

This second law applies in the same way to our behavior. The acceleration and speed at which we achieve our dreams is related to the amount of "force" we exert towards that dream. For example, writing a book could take days, weeks, months or years. This is entirely dependent on how much energy and time the author exerts on writing the book. The bigger the book (mass) the more time and energy is required to complete the book.

Obviously applying this equation will be different for everyone. But I like to refer to Newton's second law of motion as the second "Law of Dreams" motion. Understanding this law and putting it into the perspective of one's life, can make it clearer that dreams do not just happen. Dreams require action. Dreams require force and acceleration.

By understanding this second law, we can apply the mathematical principles and minimize the risk of complacency in our lives.

LAW #3

Newton's third law is known as the law of action and reaction. It states that for every action there is an equal and opposite reaction. Or, in simple terms, when two objects interact, they apply forces to one another that are equal in magnitude and opposite in direction.

For example, when we sit on a chair, our body exerts a downward force on the chair and the chair exerts an upward force on our body. There are two forces resulting from this interaction — a force on the chair (action) and a force on our body (reaction). If object A exerts a force on object B, then object B must exert a force of equal magnitude and opposite direction back on object A.

Newton's third law of motion is particularly applicable to us and our behavior as humans. Let's take for example, someone wanting to become a professional pianist. If the amount of practice the student does playing the piano, learning the skill and reading music, then the equal and opposite reaction will be an improved level of playing. Over time, the more the student practices (action) the better they become (reaction) due the effort and energy invested. Now, if the student did not practice, then there would be no reaction — and no result.

By understanding this third law, we recognize without action there is no reaction, and minimize the risk of complacency in our lives.

With Newton's laws of physics explained, it's time to move on to chemistry — with the laws of Thermodynamics. The laws of thermodynamics define physical quantities, such as temperature, energy, and entropy — and are highly relevant and applicable to our behavior. It is the first two laws that are applicable.

> *"If I have seen further it is by standing on the shoulders of Giants."*
> **Isaac Newton**

The first law states that energy cannot be created or destroyed. The second law states that there is a natural tendency of any isolated system to degenerate into a more disordered state. This law is also referred to as the Law of Entropy (or Law of Decay) which is a measure of the amount of disorganization in any type of system.

To explain this in simple terms, let's look at the following example. When putting marbles into a jar, we decide to organize them. We put a layer of red marbles at the bottom, followed by a layer of orange marbles on top, and then a layer of blue marbles. If we take this jar and shake it up, all the marbles inside the jar become mixed. We could say that the jar has now a high degree of entropy, a high degree of disorganization. To reduce this state — and put the marbles back in order — now requires a high level of energy and time.

This situation is also applicable to businesses and organizations. If business managers do not spend time and energy in their organization, it will run into chaos and disorganization. Organizational leaders need to invest energy and time into having organized systems, processes and structures so the organization can function properly and efficiently.

It is the same for us. We must counteract the second law of Thermodynamics or entropy even if it is on the shorter term. Our level of entropy or disorganization must be kept to a minimum.

> **HOW TO AVOID ENTROPY 101**
>
> - Spend energy and time on your mind, upgrading your skills and knowledge.
> - Spend time and energy on structuring your family lives and routines.
> - Spend time and energy focusing on your professional career.
> - Spend time and energy on building and nurturing your dreams and goals.

The laws of nature, whether they are laws of motion, laws of thermodynamics, laws of gravity or even the law of attraction are at work all the time whether we acknowledge them or not. Awareness is essential on how to make these laws work for our benefit and not our detriment.

Being complacent about these natural laws will only result in our future being designed for us by them. Being complacent with these laws will lead us to a life of decay.

> *"Millions saw the apple fall, but Newton was the one who asked why"*
> **Bernard Baruch**

> **THINK ABOUT**
> THE WORST-CASE SCENARIO.
>
> **ACCEPT THAT**
> AS A **POSSIBILITY** AND
> WORK ON THE BASIS OF
> — DOING —
> WHATEVER IT TAKES TO
> **STOP THAT FROM HAPPENING.**
>
> — HASSAN YOUNES

CHAPTER 14

HOW BIG COMPANIES DIED FROM COMPLACENCY

Failure happens. It is part of life, part of growth and in some cases, can be forgivable — if we learn from it. Failure due to complacency, however, is a different story.

People often say the more you fail, the more likely you are to succeed. While this bears some truth, there are many cases where this does not occur. Oftentimes, these failures are linked to complacency. Especially, in the business world.

The business world praises technology for all the doors it opens. What some people fail to understand however, is that it is a double-edged sword. It can make or break your business, and it all depends on your ability to adapt and innovate. Emphasis being placed on innovate.

Innovation is all around us. It is the single most important word in today's business language. You either innovate or copy others. In general, it is the former that creates success. However, there are cases where this is not always true. Innovators can go from winners to losers much easier than you might think. Why? One word: complacency.

Knowing that you are an innovator can make you stay in your comfort zone for too long, because you believe you have already secured your unique spot in the market. In business, this comfort zone is the last place you want to be, and it will inevitably lead to failure.

For example, look no further than Kodak. Despite the company's ground-breaking innovations, they ended up falling behind. So how did the company that invented the world's first digital camera fail to thrive in the market it created?

THE KODAK STORY

In 1975, Kodak introduced the world's first digital camera. Until then, film technology dominated. Kodak was by far the biggest player, capturing a staggering 90% market share of the US film industry.

Kodachrome, the color film that Kodak invented, was a name that resonated at the time, as loudly as "iPhone" or "Windows" would in today's tech world. Until the 90s, Kodak was always one of the five most valuable brands in the US. At the time, it seemed impossible that anything could derail the company's success. It was the undisputed king of the film and analogue camera industries and no other companies even came close.

But then the curse of disruptive innovation hit them.

Usually, companies fail as a result of not being able to keep up with the industry leaders. Kodak was the leader in the film industry, and it created the logical next-generation industry by introducing the first digital camera. Larry Matteson, Kodak executive, predicted, with accuracy, that the market segments would turn towards digital cameras. This meant that Kodak was in a perfect position to dominate the market until the competition caught up.

So, what would you do if you had an innovation and a guarantee that it would make you an industry leader? You would probably market the hell out of it, position yourself as the enviable market leader, and enjoy the spoils of your victory. But there is a complication. What if you were already an industry hotshot and your innovation could destroy your current market?

That is the position that Kodak found themselves in. Rather than leverage their unique position, they got scared of what their own innovation might do to the existing business model. So, they decided to set their innovation aside. They kept their product a hush-hush, so it would not cut into the film industry of which they were already profiting. They stuck to their core, and this kind of complacent leadership marked the beginning of their fall.

Meanwhile, companies like Sony, Canon, and Fujifilm charged ahead. When Kodak saw that they had to join the game, it was too late. They not only became followers in the market they created but also got eaten alive by the competition.

So, where is Kodak now? It is enough said that the company filed for Chapter 11 bankruptcy. Once a titan of the industry,

Kodak is now picking up the pieces and trying to restructure to stay afloat.

I believe that it is always better to learn from others' mistakes than your own, so let's look at what Kodak's failure can teach us.

Kodak made a series of bad decisions. Despite their innovations and expertize in the market, they failed to turn their idea into success. It is much better to embrace and take advantage of disruptive new technologies than to fear them.

Here are a few tips to remember:

LESSON #1

Don't Allow Success to Dull Your Edge

For too long, the executives at Kodak had the "don't fix what's not broken" mindset. Their profits were soaring and there were no serious competitors, so it seemed as if their success would never end. It is easy to get comfortable when your business is doing well. But remember that all success is temporary, especially in today's business environment. Business innovation is growing exponentially and those who don't keep up with change are finding themselves floundering or in liquidation. Continuous improvement is the cornerstone of long-term success. If you don't push it, your competitors will, which brings us to the next important piece of advice.

LESSON #2

Always Keep An Eye on Your Competitor

Many companies believe that they are immune to the influence of competitors because of their brand reputation. Kodak never thought Fujifilm would get near them. They believed people would prefer their products due to historical reputation. Of course, this didn't happen, and Fuji's strategy of offering the best value for money trumped Kodak's reputation and quality.

In the current business environment, competition is fiercer than ever. Winners and losers trade places overnight. The business world can be a tough place, your competitors will also be tough, but you have to be tougher. To build and then keep your market position, you always need to be wary of what the competition is up to. This way, you can always find a way to be a step ahead of them, to do things not only better, but different.

Apple innovator Steve Jobs didn't just compete with his competitors, he blew them sideways through innovation and fresh thinking. As he said, "You can't look at the competition and say you're going to do it better. You have to look at the competition and say you're going to do it differently."

LESSON #3

Look Beyond the Present

Many business owners are too short-sighted. They make decisions that yield short-term results, which often come with barriers to future success. This is exactly what Kodak did. Instead of investing in the future, they focused on maintaining their current success and hoped that it would never change.

Don't think of your business decisions as isolated moves. Instead, connect them into a long-term strategy for future success.

Long-term business strategies involve vision and planning. Some of the most successful businesses only focus on the long-term outcomes. For example, Unilever don't plan for short successes, they plan only for the long game and are dedicated to ensuring that their long game is both sustainable and profitable.

Some of the leading tech giants appear to be an overnight success where in fact, they all had a long-term vision.

Biz Stone, the co-founder of Twitter said, "Timing, perseverance, and ten years of trying will eventually make you look like an overnight success." Facebook founder, Mark Zuckerberg said, "Im here to build something for the long-term, anything else is a distraction." Building for the long-term is the best short-term strategy.

LESSON #4

Evolve With the Market

This is when we come to the importance of technology. It is the main driver of changes in the market. You don't have to invent any kind of cutting-edge tech to be successful. Of course, this would be the best way to succeed, but implementing existing technologies can yield equal or better results.

Modern technology should be an integral part of all your business operations. It can make your productivity skyrocket and open a world of opportunities for growth.

In addition, your business paradigm must also evolve. Everything from your business model to corporate mindset needs to keep up with market demand. When I say "market" I mainly mean the consumer market, as this is the era in which consumers decide whether your product becomes a hit or a miss.

The consumers really are the ones in charge, they are the boss, so keep up with what they want. Walmart founder, Sam Walton knew this only too well. He said, "There is only one boss. The customer. And he can fire everybody in the company from the chairman on down, simply by spending his money somewhere else."

Keep this important point in mind and evolve with the current market trends.

LESSON #5

Maintain Sharp Focus

During its golden era, Kodak did a lot of experimenting. Bathing in cash, they had all the opportunities they needed to expand in pretty much any direction they wanted. Unfortunately, they didn't take these opportunities in the right way.

Instead of focusing their investments on improving their products or expanding to similar industries, they started investing in completely unrelated businesses. These included household cleaners, newspaper editing software, and many other endeavors. Needless to say, this didn't yield the desired results. Kodak was not a leader in any of them and it resulted in a fragmented portfolio of failed attempts. This often happens when companies get complacent and don't know which direction to move in. They often try to move in all directions, but fail.

Without a clearly defined vision, this can happen to your business as well. If you plan on expanding, do it in such a way that your business creates synergy. Scrutinize every aspect of your future investment, and don't rush into this decision.

"Focus and simplicity...once you get there, you can move mountains."
Steve Jobs

LESSON #6

Don't Ignore the Signals

Had Kodak listened to Matteson's predictions, they would have probably ruled the digital camera industry. Instead, they decided to ignore obvious signs that it was time to evolve. This is something that can happen in the life of any business.

If you ever get in this situation, make sure not to turn a blind eye towards the direction of the market. Of course, this sounds much easier than it is in practice. It's not easy to analyze market needs, especially if you're in a saturated market. To deal with this the right way, it is always a good idea to invest in high-quality market analysis.

Kodak's story proves that it only takes one bad decision to ruin a successful business. It might not happen right away, but a slow death would be even more cruel. If you are an innovator in business, do not get complacent. Failure from this type of complacency is avoidable — but only if you want it.

"The shift to life-long learning is absolutely essential. As the pace of technological change quickens, we need to be sure that employees are keeping up with the right skills to thrive in the Fourth Industrial Revolution. That applies to both technical and soft skills."
Zvika Krieger

> YOU DON'T HAVE TO MAKE **GROUNDBREAKING DISCOVERIES** EVERY FEW MONTHS.
>
> YOU JUST HAVE TO **SHAKE THINGS UP** EVERY ONCE IN A WHILE.

HASSAN YOUNES

CHAPTER 15

HOW TO TACKLE COMPLACENCY

Nothing is guaranteed in life. Or business. If you recall from the beginning of this book, I explained how we live in an ever-changing world — and that applies to the world of business.

You know that first-hand. You have scrapped and clawed your way into creating a successful business.

But no leader is infallible. As you have read, any business can make the mistake of becoming complacent and ultimately losing it all. If you get too comfortable, then complacency is bound to happen.

I used the following quote at the beginning of this book, for a reason: "The most dangerous phrase in the language is "we've always done it this way.". This phrase speaks volumes. Staying in the zone of "always doing it this way" can be a limited and stagnant mindset. It can stop growth, kill innovation and cease to create new and exciting opportunities.

This book has outlined clearly, what to do — but more important, what not to do.

Now that you understand complacency, how do you avoid it? Quite simply, you must tackle it head-on. It sounds frightening I know, but the reality is, you cannot outthink it or outsmart it. You need to take immediate action.

The good news is that complacency is a human behavior. As humans, we have been equipped with the ability to change. In other words, human beings are adaptable. We can change our behavior, our patterns, habits and mentality if we choose to. The key phrase in this last sentence is "if we choose to". Before we "choose", we must have choices to choose from. But in order to see the choices that we have, we must become aware of them.

This chapter will leave you with some of the best practical tips for avoiding complacency in your life; to prevent you from sliding down a slippery slope into personal, or business failure. Sure, we can overcook strategies, or approaches, but fundamentally, avoiding complacency comes down to simple basics.

AVOIDING COMPLACENCY 101: PERSONAL LIFE

1. Prevent getting comfortable by doing something new or trying something completely out of your comfort zone.
2. Learn something new or up skill your knowledge and skills.
3. Challenge yourself by rewriting your goals, mission statement and values.
4. Change your routine by getting outside and going for a walk.

5. Embrace change by re-arranging your business strategy.
6. Avoid getting stuck by getting help in areas that are lacking for you.
7. Trying something new like reading a book out of the usual genre you read or trying a new exercise routine.
8. Reduce predictability by changing the times you do things. Wake up earlier, eat at different times, or try a new food.
9. Become ambitious by finding a new hobby or meeting new people.
10. Nurture your spiritual, emotional, and mental health by getting some professional or personal development.

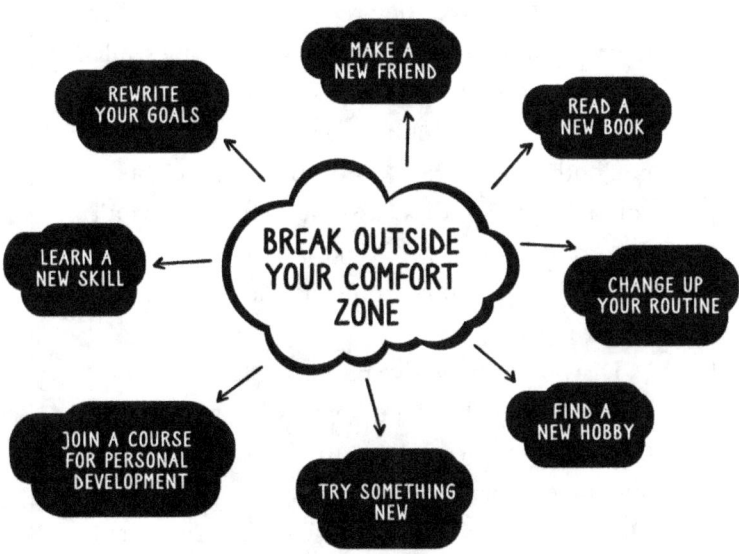

AVOIDING COMPLACENCY 101:
BUSINESS

If you are going to cure the cancer of complacency that's running through your business, these are the five actions you need to take.

ACTION #1

Start Challenging Your Team

Complacency in leadership gets reflected by your team. If your people can see that you don't really care, they're not going to bring their A-game to work. They'll skate along while doing the bare minimum. Even those who want to bring something new to the table may not bother. After all, they can see that you're complacent, so they assume that you won't make any changes. It's like a game of follow-the-leader: if you're doing it, the chances are they will too

Disrupt this negative pattern. Challenge your people to start thinking about ways to improve the business. Ask them to share their ideas and take everything that they say on board. Often, the best ideas for business improvement come from those who are on the ground. Let your team inspire you. Build a hunger for improvement within them and use that newfound energy to transform the business.

ACTION #2

Confront the Worst-Case Scenario

What's the worst thing that could happen if your business continues down its current path? If you're honest with yourself, you can already see the stagnation in progress. The revenue may not have started to fall yet, but it is also not growing. You may have your competition hot on your heels, or worse, some of your competitors may have surpassed you.

If you do nothing, more will follow. You'll go from being a leader in your niche to being an also-ran. If you don't make the changes that your business needs, you'll end up in the same situation as the printing company mentioned earlier.

The worst-case scenario is that your business collapses. Accept that as a possibility and work on the basis of doing whatever it takes to stop that from happening. Looking at the worse-case scenario may sound like a pessimistic thing to do but it's not, it's actually being realistic and understanding that some businesses do in fact fail without the right strategies and guidance. You only have to look at current business statistics to see how many businesses fail within the first five years of trade. It may be tough to look at, but it is necessary.

ACTION #3

Reward Innovation

As mentioned, your people are often your best source for new business ideas. Don't take this for granted. Build a culture of innovation within the company, for example, Richard Branson with Virgin and Elon Musk with Tesla and SpaceX, allow time and space for innovation and nurture effort over outcome.

Instead of expecting people to do the same mundane tasks over and over, challenge them to think of new ideas. When these ideas bear fruit, reward your people for their efforts. There are plenty of ways to do this. Methods include monetary compensation, personal recognition, and workplace privileges. The important point is that your people recognize that you appreciate their efforts.

As a sidebar to this, it is also important that you don't punish people for ideas that don't work out. Not every innovation will help the business. That is the risk you take when you're trying something new. If you had enough confidence in the idea to move forward with it, you can't punish the person who came up with it if it doesn't work.

> *"Failure is an option here. If things are not failing, you are not innovating."*
> **Elon Musk**

ACTION #4

Create a New Goal (And Focus On It)

When you founded your business, you knew exactly what you wanted to achieve. You had a hunger burning inside you that pushed you to work towards your goal. The business grew along with your efforts and became what it is today.

If you have lost focus or are coasting along with your business under the assumption that nothing bad can happen, then it's time to stop. The simple truth is that a business leader who has no goals won't stay in their position for long. You may have achieved everything that you wanted when you started out, but why not push for more? Ask yourself what you want to achieve now.

Do you have a revenue figure you want to hit? Focus on it and create a plan that will get you there. Perhaps you want to branch out and enter a new niche. If that's the case, do the research so you can learn about the market and what it takes to succeed within it.

You need something concrete to shoot towards or you start to lose focus. If you're not focused then you can't expect your team to know what they need to do either. A laser-focused goal will always hit its target. Focus on the bullseye.

ACTION #5

Take Responsibility for Your Own Mistakes

In trying to attack complacency, some leaders make the mistake of blaming their teams for the company's issues. Encouraging improvement and innovation within your team is important. However, as the leader, you must accept responsibility for where the business finds itself.

If your team isn't as productive as it needs to be, look at the example that you're setting.

Think back to the printing business mentioned earlier. The leaders in that company regularly took time off to play golf and laze around. They placed the burden of running the company on their team's shoulders. That is not what a leader does.

A leader constantly strives for improvement. They mentor their people and have the ability to recognize their own flaws. They know that they are responsible for what happens with their company.

The same goes for you. Take responsibility for your actions, or lack thereof, and make it clear that you are going to change. Act as the inspiration for your team.

Don't do what you have always done. Break routine, do something different. Your life — and business — will thank you for it.

FINAL WORD

There is a big difference between a leader and a visionary. People follow visions and visionaries because of passion. As a result, people fall in love with the vision of the leader — not necessarily with the leader.

If you look through history, you will notice that many of our renowned leaders who have followed their vision, have created a following — a culture — of those who have fallen in love with their vision.

A vision that has been a grounding point, a North Star, to everything they do. The life raft that has allowed them to avoid complacency and demise.

Right now, more than ever, the world needs visionary leaders. Leaders who can inspire business into pivotal change and success. Your business needs you. A leader who is strong, determined, and willing to take their business to the next level. A leader who knows how to steer the ship away from complacency and toward success. Success, that you deserve.

I hope this book will inspire you to make the changes you need to achieve that.

CHANGE
BEFORE YOU HAVE TO.

JACK WELCH

ABOUT THE AUTHOR

Hassan Younes is an international keynote speaker, widely published author and serial-entrepreneur with a background in aerospace engineering, organizational change and business management across diverse industries. He has over two decades of experience in the education and training sector.

During the course of his professional career he has worked across various industries of business management, including vocational training, travel, international education, investment and property development.

Hassan holds an honors degree in Aerospace Engineering from RMIT in Melbourne as well as qualifications in Business Administration, Business Management, Accounting, and Education.

He is the CEO of the Training College of Australia, an institute dedicated to providing practical and theory based learning for early childhood educators and nationally accredited learning for business qualifications.

Hassan is also the Founder and Chair of the International Academy of Marawi — I AM, Managing Director at Caradon Investments, Founder & Senior Business Coach for Lanao Business Services and is the Managing Director at Arndell Park Early Childhood Learning Centre.

He has been widely published both nationally and internationally on topics relating to business, success mindset, education/ skills training, business management, entrepreneurship and coaching for success.

Hassan's passion for helping shift the outlook, scope and trajectory of his clients, students and audiences is instantly recognizable, making his presentations ideal for anyone wanting to gain insight and inspiration around business, career, personal development, coaching or education.

Hassan is a sought-after keynote speaker at business, academic and personal development events and industry summits internationally.

Why Complacency Kills is available directly from Hassan, at deanpublishing.com and in all leading bookstores.

CALL TO ACTION

My name is Hassan Younes and I almost lost my business because of complacency. As a result, I now help many businesses recognize complacency, train staff and management and assist in fixing it before it destroys everything they have worked for.

You do not have to hit rock bottom like I did to benefit. Instead, I am giving you the opportunity to benefit from my expertize by taking the free online complacency quiz and then booking me for a speaking or training event at your business.

Don't let yourself get caught up in the illusion that you are not touchable by complacency. No one is immune.

I look forward to working with you.

DOWNLOAD your free quiz today at **deanpublishing.com/whycomplacencykills**

Hassan is sharing more in his INTERACTIVE book.

See exclusive videos, audios and photos.

hassanyounes.com
linkedin.com/in/hassan-younes

> **SUCCESSFUL PEOPLE**
> DO WHAT UNSUCCESSFUL PEOPLE
> ARE NOT WILLING TO DO.
>
> DON'T WISH IT WERE EASIER,
> **WISH YOU WERE BETTER.**
>
> — JIM ROHN

HASSAN'S KEYNOTE PRESENTATIONS

HOW COMPLACENCY IS KILLING YOUR BUSINESS

Complacency is the silent killer of many successful business and it can have disastrous outcomes.

Did you know that 260,000 Australian businesses shut down last year? That's right, 260,000 Australian businesses close down every year, the majority through poor leadership. Many businesses rise and fall on the back of leadership. It can be easy to lose sight of your business direction when you become complacent. Complacency can kill a business. Complacency KILLS.

Hassan's keynote presentation "How Complacency Is Killing You Business" delivers a powerful insight into his personal story as a successful entrepreneur of multiple businesses, and how he nearly went broke and lost everything, including his family. He shares his powerful "STEER an IDEA" strategy and reveals how business leaders can avoid the perils of complacency and steer their life and business in a new direction.

KEY TAKEAWAYS:

- Learn how an IDEA can immediately begin to transform your life, business or career.
- Begin to use my practical method — "IDEA to STEER" — your life, business or career.
- Learn key life-changing strategies to exponentially grow your business and yourself.

HOW TO BECOME A TRANSFORMATIONAL LEADER

In the current climate of rapid change, new leaders are emerging, and workplace cultures are changing, evolving and transforming. Now more than ever, leaders have to evolve into becoming a transformational leader in order to succeed or continue on the path of success.

As a leader, are you able to inspire others, influence their motivation and performance, facilitate a positive work culture and create an environment for development, collaboration, and innovation? As a leader, are you able to model the behaviours that your team expects from you and from others, including authenticity, courage, and vulnerability?

Your success as a leader is often followed by complacency and it can be easy to lose track of the important factors within yourself and your business/career that made it such a success in the first place.

But it doesn't have to be way, a transformational leader can turn around any business to become even more successful than before.

Hassan will share the key strategies to becoming a Transformational Leader, so you can avoid complacency and catapult your business to soaring new heights you never thought possible, isn't that why you started the business in the first place?

KEY TAKEAWAYS:

- Acquire new key strategies to become a transformational leader.
- Ignite your strengths and develop leading-edge transformative skills designed to grow your business and build a brand of influence.
- Learn how to efficiently influence your team and culture.

hassanyounes.com

ACKNOWLEDGMENTS

To the loving memories of both my parents who have raised me up to be the strong person that I am today. Who have always guided me, supported and mentored me onto the right path all my life. You are never forgotten and I know you would have been very proud of me. You are in my prayers every day.

I also dedicate my whole work of writing this book to my loving and caring wife Sarifa Alonto Younes, who has been absolutely supportive, encouraging and inspiring me in everything that I do. My wife, Sarifa, I am grateful to have you as my life partner, my best friend, my mentor and coach. You are the backbone of our success. My wife Sarifa, in my lows you always give me strength to carry on and in my highs you are always the one to cheer me on. On our wedding day I said "I do" and every day from there on I still say "I do, I do." Thank you, Hon.

To my four children Adam, Nahda, Ahmad and Dania who constantly give me inspiration, love and support. You are my blessings from God and you are source of inspiration for every thing that I do or achieve in life.

My siblings Mohamed, Ahmad, Mahmoud, Hussein and my sister Rima and their families for their unconditional love and support. I thank you for all that you have done for me and will always carry my love for you in my heart.

Thank you to all my relatives in Australia. You are all special in your own unique way and I am so blessed to be part of you all. Our special bond is what makes our family so special. Thank you for your continuous support.

To the loving memory of my dear cousin Mumtaz Younes who passed away during the writing of this book. Mumtaz you were my mentor, my guide and my adviser during my senior educational years. Your input and advice have been instrumental in what I have achieved academically. Your beautiful heart, sound advice and warm smiles will never be forgotten. I miss you beyond words can describe, and your passing is not easy to bear. Before your passing, I promised you a signed copy of this book. This is my dedication to you. Until we meet again, thank you Mumtaz.

In the Philippines to all my beloved relatives and in-laws, thank you for taking me in as your son-in-law. You all have been very loving, caring and supportive of us. I could not ask for better family to be married into. In loving memory of my father-in-heart, engineer, Mangolamba Hadji Ali who took me in as his son and whom I love like a true father. You would have loved reading this book and would been very proud of me. Thank you for the love that you have shared with me before your passing.

ACKNOWLEDGMENTS

Special dedication to Uncle Dr Ahmed Alonto Junior who always continues to inspire me through this words, affections and love towards me. Uncle Dr. Ahmed Alonto you hold a special place in my heart and I thank you for your prayers and blessings towards me.

To all my relatives in my hometown of Sibline, Lebanon, who continuously shower me with their support and encouragement. Although far apart in distance, you were never short of supporting all of my endeavors and achievements. Thank you to all my relatives in Sibline.

I would like to acknowledge Sam Cawthorn who has been instrumental in inspiring me to write this book and for providing the foreword to it.

A special thank you to Dean Publishing and their team for their efforts, support, guidance and mentoring in writing this book. Your unwavering commitment to quality, value and service has made this book such a great success. Thank to the Dean Publishing team: Susan, Natalie, Monique, Chloe, Jazmine and all the behind-the-scene members. Thank you all.

> **COMPLACENCY**
> IS MAN'S
> **BIGGEST WEAKNESS.**
> IT CREEPS UP
> ON US WHEN WE
> LEAST EXPECT IT.
>
> — JAY MULLINGS

TESTIMONIALS

"I just heard Hassan Younes speak and what an amazing message he has. Not only does he move you through powerful stories but he has also got the tools and strategies to help anyone to go from where they are now to where they really want to be."

Sam Cawthorn
CEO & Founder of Speakers Institute

"An experienced entrepreneur and excellent speaker, Hassan delivers a powerful message that we all need to hear. Hassan's insights, knowledge and strategies should be used by all businesses."

Warren Tate
Bestselling Author of
***I GET YOU – Communication can Change your Destination Coach*,**
Professional speaker & auctioneer

"Hassan shows you how not to sabotage through complacency... Just when you think everything is perfect think again!"

Catherine Molloy
Bestselling Author of
Million Dollar Handshake **and**
The Conscious Leader, **&**
Keynote speaker

"Hassan Younes is a true inspiration. He touches the very essence of our being with his personal stories that we can all relate to it. Then takes on us a journey of how we can follow his lead and turn our lives around if we just stop being complacent."

Andrea Putting
Author & Podcaster

END NOTES

1. Belsky, D. W., Moffitt, T. E., Corcoran, D. L., Domingue, B., Harrington, H., Hogan, S., ... Caspi, A. (2016). The Genetics of Success: How Single-Nucleotide Polymorphisms Associated With Educational Attainment Relate to Life-Course Development. *Psychological Science*, 27(7), 957–972. doi.org/10.1177/0956797616643070

2. Mosca, Louis. (Published online November 30, 2017) "complacent-leadership-might-be-killing-your-business". Forbes Magazine, https://www.forbes.com/sites/louismosca/2017/11/30/complacent-leadership-might-be-killing-your-business/#4ff05f3ef708

3. James, Frank. (Published online February 2, 2010). "Colgan-Buffalo Plane Crash: Errors Began Pre-Flight,". National Public Radio NPR. https://www.npr.org/sections/thetwo-way/2010/02/colganbuffalo_plane_crash_erro.html

4. Perry, Mark. (October 20, 2017). "Fortune 500 firms 1955 v. 2016: Only 12% remain, thanks to the creative destruction that fuels economic prosperity." The American Enterprise Institute. https://www.aei.org/carpe-diem/fortune-500-firms-1955-v-2017-only-12-remain-thanks-to-the-creative-destruction-that-fuels-economic-prosperity/

5. Wieth, M., & Zacks, R. (2011). Time of day effects on problem solving: When the non-optimal is optimal. Thinking & Reasoning, 17(4),387401. https://doi.org/10.1080/13546783.2011.625663

6. Norcross, J. C., Mrykalo, M. S., & Blagys, M. D. (2002). Auld Lang Syne: Success predictors, change processes, and self-reported outcomes of New Year's resolvers and nonresolvers. Journal of Clinical Psychology, 58(4), 397–405. https://doi.org/10.1002/jclp.1151

7. Etymology Online Dictionary, (retrieved July 2020). https://www.etymonline.com/word/ innovate

8. Thomson, Jeff Dr. (Sep 30, 2011) Beyond Words Blog, "Is Nonverbal Communication a Numbers Game?" Psychology Today. https://www.psychologytoday.com/au/blog/beyond-words/201109/is-nonverbal-communication-numbers-game

9. Blansky D, Kavanaugh C, Boothroyd C, Benson B, Gallagher J, Endress J, et al. (February 13, 2013) Spread of Academic Success in a High School Social Network. PLoS ONE 8(2): e55944. https://doi.org/10.1371/journal.pone.0055944

NOTES

WHY COMPLACENCY KILLS

NOTES

www.ingramcontent.com/pod-product-compliance
Lightning Source LLC
Chambersburg PA
CBHW071624080526
44588CB00010B/1261